HOW TO TALK DIRTY

Drive Your Partner Crazy And Set The Right Mood For Mind-Blowing Sex
Master Dirty Talk, Even If You're Shy and Have Taboos
(Including 100+ Dirty Talk Examples)

TABLE OF CONTENT

Introduction	4
Chapter One - Understanding the Basics of Dirty Talk	8
Chapter Two - Setting the Tone	15
Chapter Three - Decoding Dirty Talk for Introverts and Beginners	28
Chapter Four - Dirty Talk on the Phone	46
Chapter Five - Deep in the Dirty Talk	57
Chapter Six - Roleplay	66
Chapter Seven - Other Erotic Exercises	74
Conclusion	83

Introduction

It is hard enough to capture your thoughts and relay how you're feeling in everyday life – but to communicate in a way that lights up the sexual embers of your relationship? *And* keep those sexy feelings going forever? Now, that is another ball game altogether.

A lot of us encounter the problem of articulation when it comes to our feelings. It becomes even worse when it comes to communicating sexually. This goes beyond the usual "touch me here" or the more common "don't stop". No matter how sexually explicit we are behind closed doors, the second we are faced with a situation where we ought to give voice to our sexual needs, the mute buttons become activated and then everything is crickets.

If this sounds like you, don't worry about it. There are millions of people in the same boat. However, if you are ready to break out from that boring dimension and step into a colorful world where you are capable of verbally setting the course of your sexual relationship (destination: best sex of our lives), this book is exactly what you need right now and I will tell you why in a minute.

Most books or resources on the subject of 'dirty talk' tackle it from a very literal angle as the "dirty side" of your relationship. This book, "*How to Talk Dirty: Drive Your Partner Crazy and Set the Right Mood for Mind-Blowing Sex*" takes a holistic approach where it is not just dirty talk. It becomes a process that frees you to become capable of verbally expressing your relationship's sexual needs in a way that is non-judgmental, fun, unapologetic and most importantly, sexy. Your body was designed to enjoy sex but who says that it always has to be a physical process?

A single thought can awaken your body to new experiences and desires. Voicing those desires can get you to a place where your fantasies become a reality. But that is not the only reason for you to be looking into dirty talk. By perfecting this art of talking dirty, you'll be able to:

1. Improve the communication dynamics in your relationship

2. Become more sexually fulfilled in your relationship

3. Free yourself from conventional practices that inhibit you from having a beautiful sexual experience

4. Manage the physical needs of your relationship even when the distance becomes a barrier

5. Explore the boundaries of your imagination thus becoming even more creative as you grow

You need this book if you are feeling stuck in your relationship and want to remain in it but don't know where to start. You definitely need more than a few pointers if you are unsure on how to reignite the flames that made it difficult for you and your partner to keep your hands off each other. Whatever your situation, I have you covered right here.

This book, "*How to Talk Dirty: Drive Your Partner Crazy and Set the Right Mood for Mind-Blowing Sex*" takes you on an explorative journey through your senses and opens you up to a whole new world. It doesn't matter if you are the shy type or the kind of person with a tendency to get into it with "too much" gusto when communicating. There is something in this book that would either help you give voice to your inner desires or teach you to be more effective in your approach. How do I know that this is going to work? Because not too long ago, I was you.

I have been married for 12 years now but before that, we dated for seven years. I got married by 24 and if you are going by today's standards, that was pretty young. However, we had known each other since we were both 17 and even as young as we were back then, we both knew that we had found "the one" in each other. We were both smitten and eager to spend the rest of our lives with each other. As cute and beautiful as this was, it did not stop or prevent the rut we found ourselves in less than three years into marriage.

For me, it felt as though we had seen it all and done it all and the question that kept coming to my mind was "is this it?". I am pretty sure that my partner would give you similar answers if you asked. Sadly, this attitude didn't just end in the bedroom. It went on and affected other areas of our lives. We began to experience what I later came to know as "the grass is greener on the other side syndrome". It was so bad that we had a three-month separation. And it only lasted that long because I was away in another country for work. The separation made us realize that we wanted to be with each other, but we missed having that spark.

One crazy day at work, I sent my significant other a message detailing a thrilling outdoor adventure we had in our earlier years. That single message knocked down the problematic wall in our marriage and took us to a whole new level. The technology that we have today has even made it that much easier to fall in love all over again and create a more sexually exciting life.

This book documents my journey through that process and makes it easier for you to navigate those murky waters. More than that, it is a guide on improving your bedside conversation whether you are at home or at work. And it comes in very handy in helping you attain the kind of bond that you crave in your relationship. The contents of this book are applicable if your goal is better sexual satisfaction or developing the closeness that comes from intimacy. Now, I know that we set off on a very serious note. But in reality, this is all about having fun.

That said, it is okay if you feel that this may be out of your comfort zone. It is okay to be worried about all of this. But here is what I have to say. You have made it this and you can go all the way. Shed off that negative mental energy and embrace the courage to take charge. Turn over to the next page and begin the adventure that will most definitely change your life…or at the very least, switch things up sexually for you and your partner (which is pretty life-changing if you ask me). There is only one rule in this domain…have fun!

Chapter One - Understanding the Basics of Dirty Talk

Obviously, the starting point of any learning curve is having an understanding of what you are getting into in the first place. There are so many sad misconceptions and poorly conceived notions about the concept of "dirty talk". On top of my list is the idea that "dirty talk" is actually considered dirty (so wrong). In the coming pages, we will tear down those terrible notions and get you started on the right path. Some of them are going to require a lot of deliberate effort on your part to discard them because they might be things that society has drummed into your ears through the years. That is okay. Just remind yourself to keep an open mind. Now that we have gotten that out of the way, let us begin.

What Exactly is Dirty Talk?

We know dirty talk by many names; sex talk, erotic talk, bedroom lingo and so on. No matter what you choose to call it, they all mean the same thing or at least, imply the same meaning. Dirty talk in the basic sense is a sexually explicit conversation that is designed to either seduce or arouse someone. When engaging in dirty talk, you employ the creative use of graphic imagery such as erotic descriptions or sexual commands/demands to arouse and heighten the sexual pleasures of the recipient. Let me break that down. The first part of dirty talk is the intention. There has to be the intention of the sender/speaker which is to either seduce, arouse or heighten the sexual desire or pleasure of the person on the other end. It is possible for a person to become sexually heightened due to the explicit nature or sexual inferences of a conversation but if that is not the intention of the person instigating that conversation, it remains just that... a conversation.

The second part of the definition is the choice of words. They have to be sexually explicit in nature. Many of us shy away from the sexual explicitness part which is why dirty talk becomes something that we struggle with (we will get into that in subsequent chapters). However, the content of your dirty talk does not have to contain words that are considered 'vulgar' for it to qualify as dirty talk. There are ways you can use words to paint a picture that will stir up the same sexual feelings you hoping to arouse in the mind and body of the recipient and this brings us to the third part of that definition…the recipient. It is important that you have a willing participant of consensual age in that erotic chat or else, that dirty talk can easily become sexual harassment.

Dirty talk can be used as foreplay, as the main sexual act and as a way to stay connected even when there is no actual physical activity going on to implement the sexual demands. Dirty talk can be done digitally via texts, emails, chats and so. It can also be done orally over the phone, through video calls or face to face during a steaming sexual session. Dirty talk is a lot of things but dirty is not one of them. So, why is dirty talk such a big deal in our relationships?

Why are We So Turned on By Dirty Talk?

When I first discovered the joys of dirty talk, I was curious as to why I reacted this way to it. Why am I so deeply affected by a few carefully selected phrases from this person? And while we are on the subject, why does it feel so good? The answer is simple. Sex is something that we experience with more than just our five physical senses. Let me break that down for you. Back in the day, there was a notion that each gender responds to sexual stimulation. It was generally said that men are visual creatures and therefore are more moved by what they see while women require emotional stimulation which is why they respond more to how they feel. That was cute for a cool minute but thankfully, those stereotypes have been broken down and explained to us.

Women can be just as visual as men and on the other hand, men can equally respond sexually to how they feel as well. However, men have a sex drive that is stronger than that of their female counterparts and even more straightforward. Women require some kind of emotional connection to get the engines going. In essence, a man can go from flaccid to fully erect in a matter of seconds while a woman may have to navigate a longer route to get to that point where her floodgates are open. Of course, some of us experience this differently and that doesn't make you a freak. You are just the exception to the rule. Either way, unless you are one of those lucky couples whose sex drive is on the same frequency, you might find yourself juggling to keep the balance between quickies and protracted foreplay in order to make sure that the other person attains that heightened state of sexual awareness for maximum pleasure.

This is where dirty talk comes in. Dirty talk strikes that balance between being visual and having emotional content. I know that this sounds crazy but stay with me. Dirty talk is a non-physical way to create a physical reaction brought on by sexual feelings. In other words, dirty talk brings the best of both worlds together. That is one of the beauties of sex talk. The gender gap brought on by the differences in sex drive and sexual stimulations can be closed with the use of dirty talk. A well-articulated text can provoke images that can take a woman from 0 to 100 and can also get a man to keep the 'engines' revving. Dirty talk has a way of caressing your partner in their sensitive areas even when you are thousands of miles apart and this goes a long way to keeping the chemistry between you. To draw the curtains on this question, dirty talk turns us on because it combines all aspects of sexual stimulation.

The Real Reasons You're are Bad at Dirty Talk and How to Be Better

There is a very strong possibility that you are already engaging in some form of dirty talk without even realizing it. If you have ever started a conversation with the sentence… "remember that last time that we_____(complete it with the last sexual encounter), you have successfully had your foundation level dirty talk. If we are already doing this naturally, why then does this become a problem when we are expected to be more deliberate in talking dirty? I have a whole list to answer your questions.

1. Social Conditioning: There are certain words that we have been socially conditioned to regard as 'bad' so when you use such words in your conversation, it is easy to feel 'bad' about it. This feeling prompts a strong sense of guilt and shame. This is why we start out the text enthusiastically but end up sending boring mono-syllabic texts after reading it.

2. Expectations and Perceptions: You have an idea of what and who you think you and your partner should be in your relationship and functioning outside that role makes you question your sense of morals. Wives are scared to be identified as sexual creatures while husbands want to live up to that highly esteemed leadership role. Both parties feel that dirty talk would tarnish the perception that they have of themselves.

3. Lack of Confidence: I know a lot of people who can take on seemingly difficult challenges and boldly walk into a room full of people to have a conversation with them. But put them on the same bed with their sexual partners to express themselves sexually and they retreat into themselves faster than a snail. Sexual confidence is a necessary ingredient for dirty talk and without it, you are not going to make much headway.

To be better, you have to let go of the idea of who you think you are and who you think you should be and welcome the idea of exploring who you truly are. Try not to take yourself so seriously. One of the mantras you are going to have to chant consistently throughout this book is this, "I am a wonderful sexual creature, and this is my journey to exploring myself". This would help you with the "You" part of the dirty talk because one of the keys to the success of this process is you. Also, you have to remember that this is meant to be fun for you and your partner. The second it stops being fun, stop. That said, let us explore some of the things that should never be said in bed before, during and after a sexual tryst. As a matter of fact, never say them at all.

7 Things You Should Never Say in Bed

I have been guilty of a few of these things so if some of the things listed here bring to mind a painful reminder of your last verbal faux pas in the bedroom, take heart. You are not alone. Now that you know that this is wrong, you can go forward to ensure you never repeat this.

1. Is it in yet?

This phrase has the same effect as a needle on a fully inflated balloon as it does a person's sexual arousal. It implies a lot of things; one of them being that your partner is too small (if said to a guy) or too big (if said to a girl). This is one of those times where it is best to observe the situation and see how it plays out. If the size of your partner is a deal-breaker, think of creative ways to end the whole affair without bringing this up. Trust me, this is one dirty talk that can take a really dirty turn and I do not mean that in a good way.

2. Scream the wrong name

Ouch!!!! What were you thinking? Or more importantly, who were you thinking about? Screaming your partner's name during sex is a level one dirty talk move but if you do it right, you could get your partner's juices flowing. But do it wrong and you would watch that well dry up right before your eyes. People recover from this bedroom mishap, but it can mess with your sexual dynamics for a while especially if that is the name of your ex. Which brings us to the next point.

3. Make the 'ex' comparison

Yes, I get it. Your ex was a super sexy vixen or stud and your current may be lacking their skills or erm…tools but there is a reason that person is your ex. If you are still hung up on your ex so much that you are thinking of them when you should be exploring the sexual being in front of you, then it is probably time for you to stop. Reassess your current stand and make a deliberate decision to either go back to the ex or move forward with your present. Or maybe give yourself time to heal if you are unsure. If the latter is the case, ban yourself from any sexual activity until further notice.

4. Pay attention to your phone and ask to respond to a notification

Hearing your ringtone in the middle of the coupling session can mess with your mood but actually vocalizing a desire to respond to the message or call is a definite mood killer. However, this is not one of those rules that you can't get back from if you break it. A genuine emergency might require your immediate attention and your partner could be understanding about it. Just try not to make this a habit.

5. Negative Verbal Assertion

Here, I am going to go ahead and celebrate your sexual confidence as you are not shy about expressing your sexual needs. However, this backfires when you try to do this in a negative way. It can discourage your partner and make them feel like they are under pressure to perform which in turn will make their performance even poorer. Rather than stating what you don't like (save that for non-sexual situations), tell your partner what you do like. For example, "I like it when you flick your tongue on my nipples like that" as opposed to "don't suck my nipples like that". The first one has a nicer ring to it and would encourage your partner to continue doing the things that you actually like. The second one would make them stop that move or stop having sex with you completely.

6. Your Previous Sexual Transgression

There is a whole debate going on about the negatives and positives of coming clean with your partner if you cheated. I am not about to wade into those waters but I can confidently tell you this; telling them when you both are in bed and in the middle of things is not the place to do it. I am not sure what your objectives are but unless you are planning to bring the sexual relationship you have to a screeching halt, I would suggest that you steer clear of the bed for that conversation. As a matter of fact, leave the bedroom entirely.

7. Make reference about a body flaw

If you have ever done this, shame on you. However, I am just going to assume that this was the old you and after reading this, you are going to turn over a new leaf. When we become sexual, we become vulnerable physically as we risk exposing our body insecurities to our partners. Therefore, you can imagine how hurtful it would be if you throw that insecurity in their face. You may have said it with good intentions but I can tell you that on the bed in the middle of 'things' is not the way to go about it. Shut down the voice of the inner critic in your head and just enjoy the moment.

Chapter Two - Setting the Tone

One of the biggest changes I made in my bedroom this year has to be the lighting. Before now, I had this standard off and on switch which meant you either had the light on or off. You couldn't have it both ways and that was terrible because, when the light was on it was usually too bright and when it was off, everywhere was pitch black. This new lighting system I got comes with a dimmer. I had no idea how much I needed a dimmer until I installed this. It gives you different gradations of light so it goes from bright to dim to completely off as opposed to on and off. The human body kind of works the same way when it comes to sex. We are not just on and off. Although experts seem to think that most men are. Still, it requires some stimulation to get you to that "come n get it" point in the bedroom. We call this the tone. In this segment, you outgoing to learn how to set the tone for your sexy dirty talk. That way, you don't feel as though you were hit right in the face with some stuff straight out of what you imagine they would say in Playboy house. Because believe it or not people, sexy dirty talk is a process and that is what we want to get into right now.

What's Your Sexual Style?

If you are on your journey to sexual discovery and you are reading this book right now, I have to say, I envy you right now. You have the opportunity to explore your sexuality and you are doing it with a book that offers zero condemnation for something that comes so naturally to us. So it is like a very comfortable place to start. If like me you have " been around the block a few times", you already know what you want and what you like to do in the bedroom. Well, congratulations to you too. That is a well-deserved knowledge that you had gained thanks to the experiences; both good and bad. If on the other hand, you have no idea what your sexual style is, that is okay. We are here to make this discovery together. For those who think they don't have a sexual style,

I am sorry to break it to you, honey, you do. You just don't know it yet.

Your sexual style basically refers to what you like to do in bed. You may be the type who loves the cozy, warm and very intimate sex. Or you may be at the other extreme where you like to be kinky and extra adventurous in bed. There is nothing wrong with that. As long as all parties involved in the sexual process are consenting adults, you guys are fine. In a few short minutes, I will break down some of the basic sexual styles that are prevalent. But before we do that, I want to tell you the importance of knowing your sexual style. Since we are talking about setting the tone, it is important to understand your sexual style so that you can know what pace to follow. Remember the light illustration that I talked about in the beginning. Some people don't go from on to off, they need that dimmer in between to gradually introduce them to the concept of light or darkness. There are levels to sexy dirty talk. Some people may have to start from level one before they get to level two and then you follow that step by step process until you get to the highest level or wherever they are most comfortable with. For those who are of a certain kind of sexual style, they may be able to go straight to level five and then jump right up to the kinky stuff. Essentially, your sexual style tells you the pace to follow when it comes to dirty talk.

Now that we have gotten that out of the way let us look at some of the more common sexual styles.

Sexy Sexual Style:

People with the 'sexy sexual' style are often more focused on the sex and the end process than anything else. For them, sex is purely a physical act and one through which they can find orgasmic release. People in this category are very committed to doing whatever it takes to get them to where they need to get to. When they want sex, there is a sense of urgency that surrounds their approach to it. They are happy to skip the foreplay so that they can get right into the action. Because of this, they can come off as controlling and demanding at the same time. You would hardly find a person with a sexy sexual style who is weepy after sex. That is just not their thing. However, if you do find tears, most likely, it will be because they are happy from the high that the sex just provided.

For someone like this, dirty talk may never get to the "finish line" because the moment they get excited, they want to transfer all that sexual energy into the physical act. And until that happens, they would be very restless. If you are in this category, it doesn't really matter what level the dirty talk is. As long as it is able to get them to that point where they are physically excited, they are good. The only drawback I see to this is that they would never really be able to finish a sexual conversation without the physical act... and let us be honest, that is neither here nor there.

Sensual Sexual Style:

Sensual lovers have a sex style where they explore all of their five senses. Sex with them is not just a physical act. It is about genuine sexual pleasure. They have some similarities with people who identify with the sexy sexual style. Except that for them, it is more about the journey than the destination. A sensual lover would take their time making love to their partner. Sex with them begins long before there is body contact and for this reason, they are ready to prolong the foreplay. It could be a while before they get to the action and even when they get to that point, there is still a lot of exploration going on. Your sensual lover is more likely to introduce other elements into sex than people from the other sexual styles and their motivation has more to do with their love for sexual pleasure than trying things out because it is trendy. For all their sensuality and love for pleasure, they put in a lot of effort to take care of the needs of their partner but they also prioritize their needs as well.

Dirty talk for the sensual lover is one channel for them to experience sex from a mental place and you can believe that they will be down for it. As long as the conversation is able to engage their senses, these guys will follow through on that conversation for as long as possible. I believe that dirty talk with a sensual lover is bound to be very pleasurable. Mostly because they would want to be descriptive in their use of words and this would go on to tickle your imagination giving you a taste of what is to come. For a sensual lover, even the way they type "hi" in a text conversation could have double-ended meaning. Whether the dirty talk is happening physically or over the phone, it is all about engaging the senses and obtaining pleasure. However, I feel that the central level would want to build the conversation from ground up they will they would like to start from level one and then take it from there. On the plus side, there are no caps on how far they can go. These guys can take it to level 1000 if it is available.

Intimate Sexual Style:

For people in this category, intimacy is a priority. The pace of the sex is largely dependent on how comfortable they feel around their partner. Having an intimate sexual style personality does not necessarily mean that these guys are into missionary sex positions on a daily basis. You would be amazed that they could turn out to be the kinkiest of the bunch. However, the ability to explore and be adventurous in the bedroom is limited to how intimate they feel with their partner. You would not find someone who has an intimate sexual style doing just about anything with someone they have just met. They would rather want to get to know their partners. Their drive for sex is powered by the emotional connection that they feel to their partner. For them, sex is a bonding experience, not just a physical release or a treasure trove of pleasure.

Sexy talk in this situation is going to be within the confines of that relationship. How far the person goes would depend on how close they feel to their partner. In a relationship that is relatively new, it might be difficult for someone with this sexual style personality to jump into sexy talk right away. They may need to be walked through the process and that would mean starting from level one. As the trust builds and the intimacy develops, that sexy talk level would go higher. The more sexually successful a person with this sexual style personality is with their partner, the kinkier the conversation would get. And when things get really steamy between the two, you would blush if you ever heard snippets of their dirty conversations.

I am hoping that by now, you have an idea of what your sexual style is. Now, remember, your sexual style is not based on a one-time incident. You have to look at the patterns you have established over the course of your sexual history. Where you have more than three repeat patterns, that is an indication of what your sexual style is. I think I should also remind you here that there are two people (at least) involved in the sexual situation. And therefore, it is not just your sexual style that you take you should take into consideration. You need to think about that of your partner as well. If both of you have a complimentary sexual style, it would dictate the tone of the sexy/dirty talk conversation. For instance, if you find that you belong in the sexy sexual style category and your partner is perhaps in the intimate sexual style category, your sex talk would have to factor in your sexual personalities where one is more dominant than the other. And since you are naturally controlling (in this fictional scenario), you would be the one to take charge of the conversation while the other person would submit to your needs. Even if both partners are dominant, one person would still need to give in or submit to the other. So, look into how the pairing works and then let that set the tone and pace for your kinky dialogues.

7 Sexy Words to Add to Your Vocabulary

Right up to this point, I have been keeping our conversations civilized and clean. However, things are about to change and if you pay attention you could learn a thing or two. Now, this is as much warning you are going to get from me. You know what you signed up for when you made up your mind to purchase this book so, I hope you are ready for it. Some of these words I am about to introduce you to are words that we probably use on a daily basis but when you introduce them in a sexual situation, things can go from lukewarm to steamy in a heartbeat. Of course, as we go further, I am going to teach you how to use them. But for now, these are words that you should learn to get familiar with. PS: I included really good examples.

1. Hard: this is one of those regular everyday words that we use. But when you use it in a sexual context, it causes a lot of excitement. It doesn't matter if it is a man using it or a woman using it. As long as you use it well, you could elicit a "hard" response. And I think it works because it is descriptive of an act of arousal. And so when you use that phrase, the person immediately gets aroused. Let us look at some examples, shall we…

Level one dirty talk:

- I am so hard right now.
- I love it when your nipples get hard
- I can feel you getting hard
- Hearing your voice makes me hard
- Press your tongue hard on my clit

2. Wet: again, this is another everyday vocabulary that is inserted into a sexual situation to create excitement. I love the use of this word particularly because it invokes the use of imagery. Where you can see an erect penis, you can't necessarily tell if a woman is aroused until you check for her wetness. So the moment a woman tells you she is wet, there is a rush of heat that equally amplifies the arousal that her partner or the recipient of that message experience because their imagination has been put to work. Here are some examples;

Level one dirty talk:

- You are so wet and it is turning me on
- You are making me soooo wet

- I love how wet you get every time I kiss you there

- I need wet, sloppy kisses right now

- Want to get wet and dirty?

3. Dick/Cock: the word, penis, is such a clinical word that if you use it in sex, it comes out as a regular word, just in a sexual context. However, if you replace it with the word "dick" or "cock", it immediately invokes sexual desire. The imagery it brings to mind is virility. You don't hear the words, dick or cock and immediately think of something limp. No way! What comes to mind is the image of a very turgid dick and that is good for sexy talk.

Level one dirty talk:

- I want to eat your dick

- My dick is so hard for you right now

- I need a dick inside me

- Slap my nipples with your dick

- Bend me over and dick me in the shower

4. Pussy: there are so many beautiful names for the word, vagina. I have heard people call it a honeypot, a vajayjay, a cookie jar and so on. But nothing invokes the excitement of sex like the word, pussy. And even though it has been used as an insult, when you are saying that word verbally in a sexual situation, all you need to do is play a short note on the 'p' and emphasize the 's'. You will feel the heat rising. When used in a text, it invokes all sorts of nasty sexual thoughts.

Level one dirty talk:

- Lick my pussy hard and good

- You have the sweetest pussy ever
- I want you to slide that hard dick into this wet pussy
- Suck on all my sweet pussy juices
- Destroy this pussy with your dick

5. Cum: some people prefer to use the word, come. That is okay but this is not an English dictation class though. When it "cums" to sexy talk, you want to go with the word that packs the most punch and from experience (I also believe that a lot of people will agree with me on this) "cum" is that much more effective. It is the peak of sexual excitement and it brings to mind that moment. In text form, you can use it to express your sexual intention.

Level one dirty talk:

- I am cumming all over that pretty face later tonight
- Cum inside my wet pussy
- I want to make you cum
- Suck my dick and make me cum baby
- Lick all my cum juice off your face

6. Bad: now, we are back to the regular words that can also double as highly sexual words. I love the word bad so much that sometimes I deliberately go out of my way to be bad. And this is because in sex, being bad is very good. If you have a fetish for a little bit of S&M, then this is the word you can use to kick start a dirty talk in that direction. Here are some of the basic examples of how to use the word in a sexual context.

Level one dirty talk:

- I have been a very bad girl
- I want to cum inside you so bad
- Do you have a hard dick for a really bad girl?
- Bad boys deserve a good spank to learn their lesson
- Scream for me, you bad girl

7. Deep: be honest, the moment you read this word, you immediately thought of a sexual act. And that is because when used in a sexual context, 'deep' can invoke desire. For a man, he wants to be buried deep inside the woman. For a woman, she wants to feel the hardness of a man deep inside of her. And so, when you communicate this in a text, this single word captures that feeling. And even when you are using it verbally, it can take the other person over the edge.

Level one dirty talk:

- I want to bury my cock deep in your pussy
- Take me deep in your throat
- I love it when your tongue goes deep into my pussy
- How deep do you want me to go?
- Stay still. I want to fuck you in deep, long strokes

As we continue to explore the concept of sexy talk, we will add more words to your vocabulary. Feel free to be as creative as possible. The more you learn, the more you grow and the more you practice, the better you become at this.

Ways to Spice the Moment up for Dirty Talk

Initiating dirty talk can be very intimidating. Whether this is a new partner or someone you have known for years, it doesn't take out the worry or concern that things might go wrong. If this is you right now, I am going to have to stop you right there. The reason is that the moment you start thinking that things will go wrong, things will definitely go wrong. This is something that you are meant to ease into and not overthink your way out of it. Sure, it may be a new territory for you and a very scary one at that if you are an introvert. You have to remind yourself that you have made a lot of progress in this short time. Before you started this book, you probably didn't know what your sexual style is and now you do. And since your decision to go into the dirty talk terrain, you have now learned at least seven new words and how to use them in a sexual context. It doesn't mean that you should jump on the sex talk train right away though. But if you follow the step-by-step guide, you should be able to get through it in one piece.

Step One: Set the Scene

Your partner might be happy to receive a text saying, 'come and fuck me', but that doesn't really leave much to the imagination sex talk as much like having a conversation there has to be a dialogue in back and forth between you and the person you are having that conversation with and so before you jump right in with both feet you might want to put a Pause and those fingers of yours start by setting the scene if you are doing this over the text one of the quickest ways to get things started is to ask your partner where they are this would help you determine if they are in a private place where they can handle this kind of conversation with you or if they are somewhere that could compromise their job or put them in an awkward situation if the context of their texts were revealed besides sourcing out information about where they are it also gives you the chance to get your imagination to work so a typical setting the scene text message could start out like this:

- You: Hey babe, where are you?
- Babe: I am just leaving the office. I am heading home now. Where are you?

- You: Wherever you want me to be but I am hoping that later tonight, I would be inside you.

This is what it means to set the scene. With this message, you have been able to establish two things. One, you know that the person is in a safe place to have this kind of conversation with you and two, you are letting them know that you have an intention to carry on this kind of conversation. It is now left for them to take the bait and continue.

To further set the ambiance for the conversation, you can go ahead and let them know what you are wearing. Now, this creates a visual imagery in their head because they are picturing you in the outfits that you have just described. You always achieve this effect if you are as descriptive as possible. For those who are just starting out, maybe you would want to let the picture do the talking for you. You know what they say, a picture is worth a thousand words. Let the pictures do the talking. You don't have to be completely nude if that is not your thing. All you need to do is be a little bit creative. Show off a little skin while wearing something that is sexually significant to both of you. If you are a girl, for instance, you could strike a pose on the bed wearing a bathrobe. Then allow the robe to drop off one shoulder without revealing too much. This is a perfect way to say everything you need to say that you aren't ready to say yet. But also remind yourself to spice things up a little bit every now and then. However, for a first start, this is great. Consider the scene sent

Step Two: Get into Character

Through the sex conversations, both of you are taking yourself outside your daily routine and becoming the sex gods and goddesses that you really are. It is now time to step into the character. You can start by introducing what is about to happen in a non-sexual way. Is he standing at the door? Does he open the door with a loud bang or do you do the opening? Is she cooking something in the kitchen wearing your favorite outfit? These are the questions that you need to answer. And yes, it may sound like you are starting a whole movie production on a movie talking about characters and scenes. But that is what sex talk is about. It is not just using dirty words. It is about creating a fictional scenario in order to arouse both of you sexually and since it is not something that you have to physically play out right away, why not get into it completely?

Anyway, back to the character bit. This would be a great time to consider if you are going to go into role play. Are you going to be the aggressor or is that something you would rather leave for your partner? Would you like to be objectified or would you rather your partner do that? After you have cleared that out, the next thing is foreplay. How deep do you want the foreplay to be? Remember to be as descriptive as possible. Will there be kissing, touching fondling, tonguing and so on? Or are you going to skip foreplay altogether and get right down to the action? If you are getting into the action, how is the pace? Do you want it fast slow or a bit of both? Don't forget to include the sexual positions you would love to be trying out as well as. Where will you be having the sex? On the couch, on the bed or in the bathroom? This is your imagination let it run wild. While all of this is going on, be descriptive about the sensations you are experiencing. Are you wet or hard? Are you slippery and wet? You have learned some words today, use them generously.

Step Three: The Great Finish

This is the part where you cum. And just as you were descriptive and the last two steps, you would need to apply the same here. In some cases, if you have been following the conversation with some 'physical action' of your own, you may also be finding some physical release. If not, it is okay. Save everything you have just talked about for something that you can actually put to practice later.

In these three short steps, you have been able to set the scene for seduction and carry through your first dirty talk conversation. How did it feel? What was the experience like? And if you are in the same location as your sex talk partner, how was the sex after the conversation? These are things you want to explore as the answers that you get will help you grow in that area. Don't worry, the book doesn't end here. We have so much more to talk about and thankfully all of it is dirty.

Chapter Three - Decoding Dirty Talk for Introverts and Beginners

In the last chapter, towards the end, we pulled out a whole dirty sex talk conversation and for those of you who are just starting out, we may have skipped a couple of steps. Not to worry, this chapter is about helping you catch up. I am going to do that by breaking a lot of things down into easy, actionable steps.

Start Building Sexual Confidence Now

Sexual shyness stems from a lot of issues ranging from poor self-esteem to poor body image issues. And then you also have a situation where people equate their sexual performances with those of porn stars and so they expect that when they get into the bedroom, their performance will be on the same level. For starters, pornstars are not the yardstick to measure how well you do in the bedroom. These guys are professionals who are paid to act. First and foremost, you have to understand this. They are actors and as actors, they have a whole team working together to ensure that the production goes on as planned. They have directors as well as a makeup artist on set who are there to ensure that they look good. The directors ensure that the camera picks them from their most favorable side/angle. It will be impossible for them not to always look good as they do their job. And then there is the acting part. Sex is nothing like what these guys portray. If you have been comparing yourself with them, you need to create a new template for your sexual life.

As for the body image issue, I get it. We have all been there and done that. At some point in our lives, we all have some insecurity or the other about our bodies. Perhaps the boobs are not as perky as they used to be. Perhaps, you are not as endowed as you think you should be. All of these nagging issues that we have at the back of our mind could come together to compound our self-esteem problems. You need to let go of whatever expectations you have about your body. However, if you feel that it is so important to you, you can try to do something about it. Some people use surgical means to enhance their bodies. Others go on a strict diet and exercise routine.

I think the best and quickest way to get rid of any body image issues you may have is to accept yourself the way you are. You are sexy, you are feisty and you are hot. This is a fact regardless of your body size or shape. Those scars that you have on your body are there to add some decorative interest to the landscape of your body. It is all about perspective. You need to take down those negative lenses and begin to see the real you, the one that is beautiful and wonderfully made. Sexual confidence comes from knowing that you are very desirable and because of this, you are unafraid to express your sexuality. I believe me when I say this no amount of surgery or weight loss can make you feel that confident. Cosmetic surgeons who know what they are doing will ask you to see a psychologist before and after your surgery to help you build your confidence. This is because they understand that the surgery that they carry out can only fix what is on the surface. The real problem starts from within. Genuine sexual confidence starts from you accepting yourself.

That said here are a few things you can start doing today to build your confidence sexually in my opinion if you are able to conquer this territory it would reflect in other areas of your life as well because the moment we start to feel good about ourselves we genuinely begin to develop a positive opinion about the world around us and when that happens, life becomes more beautiful and adventurous.

1. Bare it all in front of a mirror
Some people may say that this is going to be too much. But I believe that you need to rip out the bandaid. Let go of the push-up bra, get rid of that tummy belt. Stop holding your stomach in. Let it all out. Stand in front of the mirror and assess yourself from head to toe. Take in everything you see with your eyes. You may not immediately fall in love with yourself, but the next words that come out of your mouth

should be these words, "I am sexy". Make this an exercise that you do every day. When you wake up in the morning, take off everything that you are wearing. Stand in front of a full-length mirror and repeat this mantra.

The purpose behind this is simple. The more you do this, the better you would begin to accept yourself as you are. Not the mental version you have created in your head based on those attachments, accouterments and the rest of it. No, this is the real you and when you accept this truth, you become more confident. Besides, how do you expect other people to find you sexy if you cannot find yourself sexy? Think about that as we proceed to the next exercise.

2. Know yourself sexually

There is this logic or way of thinking that a lot of us have and I don't understand it. We don't take the time to explore our bodies yet when we meet new sexual partners, we expect them to figure out what we want. And when they are unable to meet our expectations we become frustrated. Knowing your body sexually creates a kind of confidence that is very essential in the bedroom. Because you know what you want, you are less likely to be frustrated sexually. Also, this knowledge equips you with the courage to ask for what you want. If you are able to make your sexual demands known, there is a confidence that comes with that.

It is like going into the store to buy something. If you go without a list or a specific intention, you will find yourself wandering around the whole place unsure of what you need to get. And even when you do make up your mind about something, you would leave the place feeling unsatisfied because you never quite got what you wanted. So the very first step is knowing what you want. And then when you are presented with a sexual situation, you put out your demands on the table by letting your sexual partner know exactly how you like to be pleased. Of course, as a benevolent king or queen, you can give them room to improvise. But at the end of the day, all roads should lead to your orgasm. If you carry on with this attitude, honey, your sexual confidence will grow sky-high.

3. Wear a very sexy lingerie
This one is for women particularly. Wearing sexy lingerie can do a good and healthy number on your confidence. Even if you are not wearing it for your sexual partner, wearing it for yourself can give you that confidence boost you desire. It doesn't have to be something out of the world or something extra kinky. A plain camisole and matching underwear set can do the trick for you if that is more your thing. And if you don't have the money for it, you can still get a pair of sexy underwear without breaking the bank. All you need to do is hunt for good pieces. Mix them and match them up to create the look that you desire. It is a bonus if what you are wearing appeals to your sexual partner visually. But the main person who needs to find that whole ensemble sexy is you.

Do not underestimate the power of nice and silky underwear. Black, red and sometimes white are colors that everyone should have at least one sexy lingerie set in. However, I have seen women who were able to pull off the sexy lingerie look in pink, purple, blue and green. Do whatever floats your boat. Remember what I said when we started this list. It is all about you. The lingerie that you wear is an extension of yourself. It is also an expression of your sexuality so don't be afraid to go for exactly what you want. With so many designers and brands, you will have so many options regardless of your body size and shape. From the skinny girl wears to lingerie specifically made for thick ladies you will always have something to choose from.

While we are on the subject, you can go to the experts at the lingerie shop to ensure that you are getting the right fit for you. Your lingerie is only as good as the fitting. You don't want something that is so tight, it looks like it is cutting off the circulation in your body. You also don't want something that is too loose that it looks as if the outfit is wearing you instead of the other way around.

4. Don't take yourself too seriously

The bedroom is one place where you should allow yourself to be who you are 100% and oftentimes you need to let the silly side of you come out. This is because, sex is meant to be fun and in the end, the goal is for physical pleasure. So, why would you take sex to be this very serious thing that you need to do and show the world or at least the partner you are having the sex with that you are good. Regardless of sex (good or bad), you are good. Let that sink in as you process this information I am about to share with you. If you are too serious in the bedroom, you will reduce your chances of having a pleasurable time.

The only time I advise you to take your sex life extra seriously is when it comes to the areas of ensuring that you are taking your birth control as a woman or preventative methods as a man. You should also be serious about protecting yourself against sexually transmitted diseases because let's face it, what would suck more than being unable to display your confidence in the bedroom is if you add STDs to your list of sexual woes. Outside this, I expect you to laugh and play with your sexual partner. It is okay to laugh out loud if, in the middle of the moment, you are touched in a spot that causes you to giggle. You have not violated any laws. You have not broken any traditions. That is a simple physical reaction to something that was done to you.

Also, try not to rate your performance as you would rate other competitive sports in your life. I get it. Some of us can be very competitive. You want to believe that you are the best thing that happened to your partner sexually. Well, that may not always be the case and while that knowledge might bruise your ego, it still shouldn't stop you from having fun. Because at the end of the day, you are going to be ok. Whoever your partner was with is in the past. You need to focus on what is going on right now. And even if you have plans to stay in their future forever, that choice is not entirely up to you. Also remind yourself that no matter how amazing the sex is, you cannot manipulate them into making you that forever companion. Take those moments of sexual pleasure as they come. Enjoy the sensations and experiences but don't take it too seriously.

5. Hit the gym

Exercise as we have been told countless times releases the good kind of hormones that we need in our body. These hormones make you feel happy about yourself and when you are happy about yourself, you would feel more confident. Apart from the release of happy hormones, exercise is one way for you to take charge of your body. Where it becomes a problem is when you are expecting results to happen overnight. Having unrealistic physical expectations is one of the reasons a lot of us quit our fitness routines. We feel that running on the treadmill for one minute is enough to shed off all the fat you gained from last year's Christmas dinner. This is not how it works.

You need to combine a healthy diet routine with your exercises as well as the expert opinion of fitness trainer and nutrition is in order to see some results. Now, not all of us can afford to have personal trainers and nutritionists on our payroll. It doesn't mean that enjoying the benefits of physical exercise is out of it for you. With a little bit of online research, you could come up with information that is valuable to you and with a little commitment and consistency you can come out on the other side better. However, let us put all of that aside and focus on the facts of the situation. A workout is good for your body. It is also good for your mind and when you have something that's good for your mind and your body, the payout is often in your confidence. In this case, I would say it's a win-win situation.

There are so many other things you can do to build your sexual confidence. Things like sharing your sexual fantasies with your partner, engaging in activities that bond two people together (which is exceptionally good for people who are of the intimate sexual style category). I would have loved to list all those things out here but that would mean an entire book on its own. So instead, I came up with this idea for an assignment. Think of the things that I have shared with you so far. Review them and then every week, read up on something new that you can add to this list. More than reading about it, I would like you to act on it. Knowing something is one thing; acting on the information that you have gotten is another thing entirely. You are bound to get the results you desire if you take action. So, even if you decide to stick with just these five confidence-boosting tips I have listed here, ensure that you are consistent. Keep practicing them until they become a habit that now becomes a part of you. I wish you all the best.

Step One: Getting Good at Flirting
Flirting is a form of sexual banter and if it is done with your sexual partner, it can do wonders for your confidence. For starters, it feels good to be made aware of the fact that someone is into you. But more than that, it can inject some fun and excitement into your sexual life. Flirting is also a precursor for dirty sex talk. A lot of what goes on in the conversation when you are trying to talk dirty is flirting. Again you need to get rid of the misconception that dirty sex talk essentially involves the use of all the words you are not allowed to use on daytime TV. It is more than that. It is an exchange of sexual ideas and energies that do not involve the actual act. However, it engages your mind in such a way that you experience an intensity of sensations that can rival the actual sexual experience from physical activity. This is why people love doing dirty talk.

It would interest you to know that despite the fact that flirting is somewhat biologically programmed in us, many of us are late bloomers. And by us, I am also including those of us who have been crowned the Masters of flirting across the zodiac system astrologist (hello Sagittarius). It would seem that either they are lying, or we missed out on some of the important genes during the creation process because we cannot even flirt to save our lives. but not to worry in a few short steps I would share with you on how to become better in the art of flirting.

1. Use your eyes
They say that the eyes are the windows to the soul. When it comes to the game of flirting, you can use your eyes to open yourself to your partner in a very sexual way. This would require you to understand the fine art of body language. If I lost you there for a minute, I apologize.

Let me retrace my step and get you back on track. The most primal form of communication has always been body language. Before you were able to utter your first words, you had the ability to communicate your needs and wants to your parents. Of course, a lot of it came in the form of cries but then again, there were moments where certain gestures were interpreted accurately to mean something that you needed.

As we grow older these, gestures become more articulate. Even though we are more reliant on spoken word, there are still subtle things we do with our bodies that pass a message across. Before we get into the bit about using the whole body to flirt, let us focus on the eyes. If you happen to be one of those people who were blessed with really expressive eyes, I would say lucky you. If you are like me (with the regular eyes), there is still so much you can do to work with what you have. Besides, there are all these features on your face that can play a supporting role in helping you pass the message across with your eyes.

Before you jump into making pouty faces and batting your eyelids at a complete stranger, let us start with the basics... a gaze. There are ways that you can look at someone that would make the person feel as though they are naked. Sometimes, it is not just about how rapidly you are blinking and batting those eyelashes. It is how long you hold that gaze. Say you are in a room full of strangers and this hottie is looking at you. Holding their gaze for longer than five seconds says you want to talk to them. This is one of the most basic steps when it comes to flirting.

If you are in very close proximity with the person you are flirting with (as in shoulder to shoulder), or say you are trying to flirt with your partner (the one who you will be having all these dirty sex talks with), the best and most effective way to flirt with them using your eyes is to keep your eyes on their lips. That look essentially is communicating to your partner and telling them that, "you want to get busy with them" without so much as saying a single word. To amp things up for better impact, try this simple trick. When you know that the person you are flirting with is aware of what you are looking at, lick your own lips slowly.

2. Let your body brush up against them "accidentally"

Whether you are flirting with your partner or a complete stranger, the accidental brush is always a great move to make. If your flirting has progressed from the both of you being a few feet away to standing beside each other, the next thing to do is to allow your body brush against your partner's ever so delicately. There is no specific technique to this per se. I think that the golden rule to remember here is to ensure that this brush is as gentle as possible. No shoving; that is like kindergarten stuff where you rough handle the boy or girl you are interested in (phew, children). What you need to do is pretend as though you are walking past them (if they are not too close to you) or reach past them to get something (if they are beside you).

If you are going with the former, as you walk past them, gently move your body in a way that a part of you touches them as you move. The same thing should happen if you are reaching past them to pick up something. And when the touch happens, if you are feeling bold enough, you can acknowledge that touch with a follow-up gaze like the one we just learned recently. Look back at them as you leave (or return to sitting position) and then continue with whatever you are doing. In a more familiar setting where you know this person, you can engage them in an adult game of footsie under the table. I love this kind of flirtatiousness, especially when it is in a very formal dining setting. So picture this; you guys went out on a fancy date and you are at the table having a casual conversation as you are waiting for your food to be served. on the surface, this looks like a normal beautiful date however underneath the table something steamy is going on. Gently slide in your foot out of your shoe and then trail your partner's leg with your foot slowly, deliberately and sexually; all the while keeping a straight deadpan face as though nothing is happening.

Again, if this move seems a little too bold for you, you could go for the more direct but very subtle and delicate touch. In this case, when you are talking to the person, you include your hands in the conversation. All you have to do basically is touch them on their hands, their arms or perhaps use the excuse of getting something out of their hair to touch their hair. Don't do all of this at once though because then you can become too much. This kind of flirting is not very pronounced like the other two but it is also very effective. It immediately creates an intimate atmosphere that can easily become sexually charged. However, there are a few rules you must abide by. You should ensure that your touch is not on places that are considered inappropriate for instance if you must place your hand on their leg you have to ensure that your hand is not going above the knee as that is considered too intimate (unless of course, you are already intimate with that person). Your hands-on their arms should not stroke does not mean you should stroke the length of their arm unless of course (you guessed it), you are familiar with them. Generally, any touch you make should not linger unless there is an already established familial relationship between the two of you. Outside this, you can go ahead and have fun with this.

3. Playful Banter

Now, this is the kind of flirting that can happen whether you are having a one-on-one conversation with the person physically or you are chatting with them over the phone. It doesn't matter if it is a voice conversation or text conversation, flirting with words is an essential ingredient for any relationship, at any stage and can act as a precursor for dirty sex talk. The difference between playful banter and the actual sex talk is that when you are having a playful banter, it is an exchange of wits. Both parties are just trying to be funny and playfully tease each other. On the other hand, when you are having a sex talk, you both have the motive of sexually charging things up.

And so, when you are having a playful banter, your conversation is not always inclusive of sexual connotations. Although they could be implied phrases and sentences, nothing is ever definite. However, there is a way that the conversation can flow during the playful banter that it can come across as though you are laying the foundation for the sexy talk. It is interesting how something innocent can lead to something beautiful. For people with their different sex personalities, as we discussed in a previous chapter, you will find that this playful banter works with almost every personality type. Whether you are the sensual, sexy or intimate sexual personality type, you would appreciate what playful banter brings into the relationship.

As long as certain boundaries are respected, I would say that playful banter is the most effective way to flirt. Some people engaging in playful banter would not even realize that they are flirting with the person they are talking to. That is how easy it is and just as non-committal it feels. The only downside would be the fact that when you fail to respect boundaries, what you feel is playful teasing could be hurtful to the other person. So, it is important that you understand the nature of the person you are having this playful banter with. If they are very sensitive, you need to keep it gentle. And even if they are not sensitive, you have to understand that there is a line between playfully teasing a person and taking verbal jabs at a person's insecurities; that is just mean.

To wrap this segment up, I would say that effective flirting comes from a place of comfort. If you are not comfortable carrying out these activities, it could show and not everyone finds that appealing. You have to be confident when you flirt. Or at least, act as though you are. This is one of those moments where you fake it until you make it. If you are in a relationship with the person you are flirting with, there is a very strong chance that you are already comfortable with that person and so flirting could come easily to you. When you decide to flirt, you could choose to go with just one of the things I have listed here or you could go with all three in no specific sequence. The common social anecdote today is, "do you" and when it comes to flirting, whether you are flirting with your partner of several years, your new boyfriend/girlfriend of a few months or someone who you are just getting to know, the bottom line is, do you.

5 Starting Out Tips for All Beginners

In the beginning, talking dirty might feel very awkward whether you are a guy or a girl. If your partner is interested in taking your bedroom conversation to another level, I can understand the trepidation you feel. This is not the kind of conversation we have on a daily basis and no one ever really is groomed in the art of sexual communication. But then again, you also feel this excitement because the idea of talking dirty in such a sexual way can be a turn on. Well, there is a long list of things you can do to get things started in that direction, thankfully. However, I am going to start with the one thing you are not going to do. You are not going to jump from A to K in the art of talking dirty. Instead, you are going to follow the process. While you may have an inclination for dirty sex talk, it still makes a lot of sense for you to go through the process to help you build intimacy as you unleash your inner desires.

You have already gotten some amazing tips from the previous chapters with classic examples of level one dirty talk. This bit is about putting you in the mindset to initiate or respond to this new dimension of conversation with your partner.

1. Be confident and flirt a little

These are two different steps but I put them together because we have already covered this in-depth before. As you know by now, these are the foundational steps for getting into the dirty sex talk program. confidence helps you get over any mental blocks you may be having. The more confident you feel, the more creative you will become as you are more comfortable trying out new things. Confidence also allows you to be vulnerable without feeling anxious. That is not to say that each time you initiate, you are not going to feel that twisted ball of anxiety but confidence helps you get through it. However, if things are feeling a little too intense, being flirty can lighten the situation. Let us not forget that flirtiness also boosts your confidence. When you are just getting started with this whole sultry lingo for the sexual explorer, you need to come from a place of seduction. And seduction dear friend is born out of flirtatiousness. If nothing else, being flirty helps you retain your sense of humor. That way, even when things go horribly wrong, you can still bounce back with your confidence intact.

2. Turn on the sound in the bedroom

During sex, the sounds that we make can be a major turn-on for our partners. If you are the silent type, perhaps it is time to raise the volume a bit. Nobody said that dirty sex talk has to be coherent or written by a 15th-century lothario. The sounds that you make are inspired by the pleasure that you feel. In other words, you are voicing your pleasure. Perhaps this is why it appeals to our sexual partners. They are made aware that whatever they are doing currently is providing immense pleasure. This instills a sense of pride in them and in the heat of the moment, it can intensify the connection. While I encourage you to be a little louder in the bedroom, I urge you to do it from a place of comfort Do not attempt to replicate the same sounds that you heard of that porn video simply because you think that that is what sexy should sound like. Also, if the sounds you are making are distracting you from actually enjoying yourself, that is a sign that you are acting. In the beginning, as you work on your bedroom audio, it may feel like acting. But only if you focus too much on what you sound like. Little sounds of pleasure are all you need to get things started. Remember, the idea is to make you more vocal about your pleasure.

3. Take it easy on the use of profanity

This one may come as a shock to you but dirty sex talk does not necessarily mean that you have to use profanity. If you or your partner have an aversion for curse words, there is no point using them in your dirty talk as that would not be in any way or form appealing. However, this does not have to mean that your talk will not pack the same sexual intensity because of the absence of profane words. Here are a few examples to show you what I am trying to say;

Level one dirty sex talk [x]:

- I can't wait to rip off your clothes when you get home
- Your hands-on all my sensitive spots is all I can think of right now
- Be naked when I get home. I have some plans

Level two dirty sex talk [xx]:

- I love how tight and warm you feel every time I am inside you
- The way you alternate between licking and sucking my nipples makes me extra wet
- You can do whatever you want to do with me baby

Level three dirty sex talk [xxx]:

- I want to come home and sit on your face
- I will suck all your juices out of you later tonight
- I want you on your knees with your mouth open so that I can ride your face
- I loved how you screamed as I fucked your ass last night

In all the examples I gave here, none of them employed the use of profanity and this just goes on to show that you can have a dirty sex talk that is, um, clean. The main ingredient is your ability to express yourself sexually in the most creative ways.

3. Set clear and firm boundaries

In my research for this book, I was surprised to find that a lot of people feel that exploring your sexual dialogue means little to no rules. This is so wrong. Boundaries place you within your comfort zone so that you can safely explore your limits without feeling as though you are being violated. For example, while some people may be comfortable with the use of derogatory sexual terms during your dirty talk conversation, others may not. Dirty sex talk is an avenue to explore aspects of your sexual life but under no circumstances should you be made to feel bad about it. The second you start to experience anything but pleasure and joy, you need to step back. It is like exploring things in the bedroom. If things are not as steamy as you hoped and you begin to experience pain (and do not derive any pleasure from the pain), that is a clear sign that you need to stop and reassess your strategy. Have a nice and long talk with your partner. Go over the stuff that you are comfortable with. Come up with safe phrases that you can use to let the other person know that they are crossing lines. Don't allow yourself to be coaxed into doing what you don't want to do. Be clear. Be firm. Be focused on satisfying your sexual cravings and curiosity.

4. Start your dirty sex talk over texts

Text messages offer some form of anonymity which allows you to be more expressive. Obviously, you know who is behind the text messages but the absence of your physical presence means that you can eliminate that sense of judgment. You can hesitate to respond without coming off as weird and yes, you can make weird faces at the messages that you receive without your partner ever knowing about it. Because believe it or not, your partner is going to send some things that might catch you off guard and vice versa. In a real-life one on one situation, those revelations would probably be followed by awkward silences. Over text messages, you give yourself and your partner some time to ruminate over the ideas and then get used to the concept. This would also give guys enough time to come up with your own witty or saucy response. Just be sure to double-check who you are sending the messages to. We all know that with one button, a message for one could easily become a group thing and you definitely do not want to go there. And one more thing, ensure that you are doing your texting in an appropriate environment. In the middle of an important boardroom presentation is not one of those places.

5. Be descriptive during foreplay

Now, you are taking the dirty sex talk offline. It is no longer about discussing your fantasies. Here, you are vocalizing your anticipation. You do not need to vocalize the whole event but be descriptive of what you are expecting occasionally. A little "pull my hair, bite me there" and so on can get things going in that department. Again, you do not need to rate your vocal skills with that of a porn star. Go for what you are comfortable with and speak from a place of pleasure. If you are so distracted by the things that are being done to you (which you will at some point), staying coherent might become difficult. But that does not need to get in the way of things. Remember we talked about making sounds in the beginning. This is where that can come in really handy. Moan and groan where you need to say something but can't seem to find the right words. This does not need anything fancy...oohing and ah-ing appropriately would suffice. If on the other hand, your words are not directly affected by the steamy action taking place, that is even better. Now you can use your words to direct the flow of events. Start by telling your partner what you want them to do to you or what you want to do to them. When you do this, bear in mind that you don't need to make lofty promises. Focus on what you are doing at the moment. You can start by talking about how you want to take off their clothes, kiss them on their neck and then let things progress from there. I should also chip in here that it is not just about what you are saying. Don't get me wrong, what you say matters. However, the real deal here is in how you say it. The way and manner in which you phrase certain words can take your conversation from 0 to 10 in a matter of seconds. Again you don't need to sound like anyone else but yourself. Just allow yourself to experience the moment and then let the words and how you say those words come from what you are feeling in the moment.

6. Use complimentary words during sex

At this point, dirty talk is no longer about what you want to do to your partner or what you are expecting to be done to you. The focus here is on what is being done to you. You might be tempted to get a little critical about your partner's performance, especially if you are not getting the feelings of pleasure that you were expecting. From my personal experience and I believe the experts would also support me on this, you need to be more vocal in encouraging your partner. In trying to do this, you should not become a cheerleader. This is because, it may come off as condescending. This is also another one of those times when it is not just about what you are saying. It is how you say it. Also, avoid using negatives at this point. So, instead of saying don't touch me there, be subtle in evading the touch on that area you don't want to be touched. And when you do get touched in the right way, be vocal in expressing your approval. As I said earlier, you don't have to go to the cheerleader route. Simply saying, "that feels good" instead of, "you are doing it right" is more effective when it comes to continuing the dirty sex talk conversation. The latter makes it feel as though they were doing something wrong in the first place and in the bedroom during sex is not the best time to pass that information across. This is all about pleasure and sustaining that positive energy throughout the entire experience.

7. Don't be bothered by the silence if it happens

If either or both of you are just getting used to the concept of dirty sex talk, you should expect those awkward silences. This does not necessarily mean failure. It just means that one of you (or possibly both), would need some time to adjust to this whole process. Silence is a perfectly normal reaction to a conversation you are not used to having. When it happens, what both of you need to do is to pause and then reflect on the experiences that you have had so far. If anyone is uncomfortable with any part of it, this is the time to let the other party know. That said, from the first point that I made when I started this list to this very point that we are right now, I would say that the most important thing for the success of engaging in dirty sex talk is ensuring that the line for communication is always kept open. More than this, there is a need to ensure that both of you feel safe enough to discuss your desires and manage your expectations without feeling as though you are being judged or worse, criticized. As long as that safe space is there, even awkward silences can be laughed away.

Now that I have given away my best tips for getting into the zone for dirty sex talk as a beginner, I should point out here that the key to all of this lies in how you manage the expectations or both you and your partner's. If you are looking for a way to fix something that is broken in your relationship and you think that dirty sex talk will magically make that go away, you are wrong. Dirty sex talk is not a tool that will magically make those problems disappear.

Another expectation that you need to keep to the minimum is the thought that everything is going to proceed perfectly. I hope that you are aware at this point that there is no such thing as perfection. To enjoy this process, you just need to embrace the moments from the shocking revelations (which you are going to get a lot of) to the awkward silences which might happen occasionally. Remember, you are not trying to become the next pornstar. And so, if your messages are not looking or sounding the way you hoped they would, it is okay. As long as they are reflecting your needs and desires, as well as that of your partners and you both, feel comfortable with this whole thing, I would say kudos you are doing a great job. In the next chapter, we are going to take things to the next level.

Chapter Four - Dirty Talk on the Phone

If you are shy and you identify as an introvert, taking your desire for dirty sex talk to the phone is the perfect place to start. In the previous chapter, I did talk about phone conversations providing you a certain level of anonymity. But the benefits go beyond that. When you are having sex talk on the phone, whether you are doing it verbally or through texts, you have more options. The phone gives you the ability to animate your conversations and make it that much more interesting without having to deal with the awkward silences that we talked about earlier. No doubt, there will be awkward silences during phone texts, but it is not as intense as when you experience it during a one-on-one session. And since you are a beginner, text messages offer you a variety of ways to spice up your conversation. One of my favorite things about text messages is the use of emojis. Those characters bring life to the message that you are trying to pass across. If you are the kind of person who is used to sending plain text messages, this is a perfect time to get used to your emojis. And if you are creative enough, throwing in some gif characters can make a lot of difference. In this chapter, we are going to explore how to initiate dirty sex talk over the phone. You would also get great tips on how to keep things interesting. More importantly, you would be getting a lot of examples to guide you.

The Secrets Behind Sexting

For those who do not know, a sext is a text message with an expression of sexual intent. If you have ever sent a message to a person saying, "I want you now", you have sent a sext. Of course, that would depend on the context in which you sent that message. Still, it has a sexual connotation and from the other end, when there is no explanation beyond what you just sent, it will be safe to say that this is a sext. Putting all the analysis aside, exchanging texts with a person who wants you just as much as you want them can be the most exciting thing in a relationship. It doesn't matter if you are exchanging those text messages from across the room (which can be super sexy), or across the country (which also brings some steam into the relationship) using your modern-day device that has become a very important part of your lives to communicate about a bonding activity like sex can be super enriching for any relationship.

When you are having a verbal communication on the subject of sex and I am not talking about it from a clinical perspective (who wants to do that anyway?), talking about getting frisky and a little bit freaky with your partner using dialogue, you might experience this panic. And that is because you are wondering what to say. Switching to text messages allows you time to process what you are feeling and also to creatively come up with responses to your partner's messages that are equally just as scintillating. I understand your worry about not knowing what to say However, there is something I need you to understand. In this book, I could give a thousand sexually charged sentences or phrases that you can use as examples. But to be honest, they wouldn't really help you because you are the one in your situation you know what your body wants. You know what you need. You just need to find a way to say those words and the smartphone in your hand could be the perfect tool to express your sexual desires.

Since we have established that sexting is really about what you want, this is the point where you ask yourself this very pertinent question, 'What do you want?'. Of course, we know that you want your partner or perhaps you want to improve your sex life. But those are not the answers we are looking for here. At this point, we are trying to establish what your sexual needs are. And so, you should be thinking more in the direction of answers to questions like, do you want your nipples to be played with more? Would you like to engage in more penetrative sex or oral sex? If you are having sex in public, what are the elements would you want to include in that scenario?

Now, these are the kind of questions you should get answers to. Obviously, if you are not the kind of person who pays attention to your own needs, you may not immediately know what you want. So, it makes sense that for a start, you initiate that sex talk with yourself. This is so that you are better able to communicate what you need. If you don't know what you want, how do you express your sexual desires? Many of us have this habit of reading things off the internet or paying attention to what our friends tell us about what they think is appropriate in the bedroom and without really making our own assertions, we take this as the norm for us. And this ends up becoming a problem because, as I said earlier, you are the only one who knows what your body needs and to fully explore those needs, you need to get to know yourself more in a very sexual way. That is the secret to excellence sexting. So, how do you get to know yourself? I have got five tips for you to put into practice and you will master your body in no time.

1. Start a sex journal

A sex journal helps you keep track of your sexual journey. It helps you document your thoughts, your feelings as well as your desires. For those of us who are afraid of writing, this should not scare you. You are not writing an essay that would be assessed by your professors. This is for your eyes only. Grammar is not what is important here. What matters is that you are putting down your true thoughts. Try as much as possible to be very honest with yourself. There is no need to play coy. Say it as you mean it. The more honest you are with yourself, the better you will get to know yourself. For me, I find it easier to write in my sex journal when I start the sentences with, " I like it when…" This helps me focus on actual sexual experiences as opposed to things that I think I want. In the same vein, I use the negative to express the things that I don't like. So instead, I say, "I don't like it when…". This is not exactly the witty repertoire we hope to find in a sex journal but it works well to help you get to know you better…sexually. Try it. You might be surprised.

2. Watch porn

Yep. I said it. Porn watching is not an activity best left to pervs who have no life. If watched with deliberate intention, you can use it to discover the kind of things that excite you even though they are things you haven't really tried out before. You have to approach it with an open mind though. You might be skeptical about some of the techniques used and some of the terrible acting involved but remind yourself that you are not there to analyze and critique their performance. Your job is to observe and experience those sexual scenes virtually. You would have to be a little bit analytical in your observation. Ask yourself questions like, what turned you on? Why did that turn you on? What would you like to try sexually from the video that you just watched? The answers that you get would make a great addition to the content that you already have going on in your journal. As you make porn a part of your journey to sexual discovery, remind yourself that you are not trying to become the next pornstar. You are only there to get pointers on what turns you on and not trying to become someone else. This is very important.

3. Masturbate

If you haven't started getting physical with yourself, I urge you to begin. Those solo expeditions can help you understand your body in ways that would positively impact your sexual life. Some people have a lot of reservations about masturbations and this can cause a mental block when they try to explore their bodies. At the beginning of this book, I talked about some of the misconceptions people have about dirty sex talk and one of them was about our attitude towards sex generally. We overlook the fact that sex is a part of our biological programming and it is how we experience maximum physical pleasure. My point is, sex is a very natural part of you. And ideally, we should be able to meet sexual partners who understand our bodies and know how to please us in the sack. But in reality, even with experience, many of our partners would stumble around in the dark and that is because they don't know. The only way they can attain that knowledge is if they are very experienced, very observant and very open to your needs. And that would require time. The quickest and most effective way is for you to provide guidance and sexual exploration through masturbation is the way to go. Another bonus is the fact that it would give you a lot of material for your dirty sex talk.

4. Create sexual fantasies

This is kind of like writing a journal, except that you are taking things a step further. Here, you are building on the things that you like and using that to create an ideal sexual scenario that is built entirely on your fantasy. This is something that you would be the only one to read so you can afford to be as elaborate as you can. The more descriptive you are in creating your sexual fantasies, the better equipped you will be when you begin sexting. I feel that because your fantasy contains all the elements of your sexual desires, it gives you deeper insights into what you are craving. Which is perfect in getting you to where we want you to get to...becoming more vocal about your needs which would play out in your texts.

5. Start practicing

Practice makes perfect they say and if you want to become better at sexting, you need to start practicing. Hopefully, everything you have learned from the last three steps can provide you with enough insight on how to begin. But, if you are still in the process of figuring that out and you want to get right into sexting, you can take pointers from the samples of messages that will be shared in every chapter in this book. You don't have to copy the texts word for word but you can let them inspire your inner deviant writer. Sexting is not about being the most eloquent writer. It is about being good about describing what you want to your co-sexting mate.

5 Insanely Fun Sexting Games

If you look at the serious introduction that I gave to the subject of sexting, you would be forgiven if you assumed that the entire process is clinical. On the contrary, sexing is all fun and games. As long as you are able to nail the communication part right, you should be just fine.

Thankfully, the previous segment provides all the practical information you need to make that happen. Right now, we are going to focus on some of the fun ways you can incorporate sexting into your sexual repertoire. These games are a perfect way to get you into the spirit of things without really going requiring you to become a "sexpert". The best part about it for me is that they can help you build your sexual vocabulary without the pressure of being good at what you do.

1. The Memory Game

This game is about taking a trip down memory lane, except this time, you are focusing on your sexual escapades together. It is a variation of dirty sex talk that focuses on sexual experiences you have enjoyed while hinting at what you would most enjoy and hope to be done to you. The intent here is to use the good old memories that you have had together to build new good sexy memories. There are so many benefits to taking a trip down memory lane. For starters, it has a way of renewing those spicy sexual flames associated with the early part of any relationship. It brings you back to those days when you couldn't keep your hands off each other. The second thing I love about this game is that even if you are just starting out as a beginner when it comes to sexting, you have a lot of material to keep things interesting. So, how do you play this game? You start things off with the phrase, "Remember when…" and then fill in the dotted line with a descriptive narrative of a sexual event that was very pleasurable for both of you. In this game, you are meant to give teasers with open-ended questions so that your partner can fill in the rest of the puzzle. There is only one major rule in this game. The trip down this sexual memory lane is limited to experiences shared by both of you. In other words, there should be no talks of the exes.

2. The Emoji Guessing Game

The emoji game is exactly what you think it is. It is a game of emojis. Except, in this case, you find a way to take those cute characters and try to get or give the dirtiest meaning to them and then ask your partner to guess the meaning. The game could start out with a theme. Say you want to make it about sex positions to try out later. So, what you do is string up a set of emoji characters together that you feel best describes what sexual position you are hinting at. To make it more fun and a little more difficult, limit the emoji characters in each text to five. Each time you play the emoji game, you can always come up with a new theme and new ways to keep things fun and interesting. Increase the stakes so as to motivate each other to keep playing. Something like a nice sexual favor if they are able to guess the meaning in three attempts would make most people willing to keep going at it. Come up with creative offers that would cause your partner to salivate and drool.

3. The Orgasm Race

This is the adult version of that 'race you to the door' games we used to play as kids. It was fun back then but it is even better now. In this scenario, the door is an orgasm and both of you race each other to see who reaches an orgasm first or last (this depends on what the rules are and what is at stake). The fun part of this game (besides the orgasm that is waiting for you on the other side) is the fact that you would have to update each other via texts every step of the way. You can use texts or images to let each other know where you are on the race to orgasm. This is the most important part of the game. Take saucy images of various parts of your body as you go through the various stages of arousal. Tell your partner what you are currently doing to yourself to get to orgasm. Be as descriptive as possible. You want to use words or images that you know would turn your partner on and perhaps, get them to orgasm faster. You can prolong the process to build anticipation. Either way, when orgasm is the goal, there are no losers. This is a classic win-win game and who can resist that?

4. The Story Puzzle

Have you ever heard of those couples who have become so close that they complete each other's sentences? Well, we are not trying to become those people. This game is about getting you guys to complete a sexual fantasy with your words. One person starts off the game with a single sentence and the other person picks up from where they stop and this back and forth continues until you have a complete story. At the end of the story, when you guys get to see each other physically, you act out every bit of what you have written. You can choose to write the story in a first-person narrative or third person. Mix it up every other time to give room for role play. All that you need here is a little bit of creativity. It is also a way to carefully create sexual fantasy that you can act out and I think the fun part is the fact that both of you are creating this fantasy together. Remember, every single line must be acted out according to the script. From the props to the dialogue, the reenactment of your sexts must be accurate. So, bear this in mind when you try to fill in the blanks of the story you are creating together. Have fun!!!

5. The Remote Control

This is a sexual variation of truth or dare. Through the texts that you send to each other, you remotely control their actions. For couples with the dom/sub dynamics in their relationship, this is perfect. Even if you are not into that sort of thing, you can still have fun with this. The sexts in this game are basically an exchange of instructions from one party followed by proof of action being carried out by the other party who then delivers their own instructions. The instructions are usually of a sexual nature. Failure to comply could result in the non-compliant partner submitting to a sexual favor for the instructor. Personally, I find this game perfect for foreplay. Examples of instructions in this fun sexting game could be something like;

- Take off your panties and stay commando for the rest of the day

- Go to the restroom, open up your bra, grab a boob and flick your tongue over your nipples

- Bring out your dick, do a slow up and down stroke three times and then stop

As you continue to keep your sexting lines open, you would come up with new ways to play with your partner. Hopefully, these games I have shared offers you new ideas. In the next segment, let us look at what the phone sexperts have to say about this.

Must-Know Advice from Phone-Sex Experts

When you want to veer into unfamiliar territory, who better to help you get into the swing of things than the pros themselves? For this particular segment, I had to talk to people who offer their voices for phone sex conversations professionally to give us pointers on how to become sexperts in our own phone sex conversations. This chapter is particularly focused on having dirty sex talk through text messages but we know that we do a lot of voice calls too. It makes sense to reel that into this conversation since we are on the subject. Whether you are thinking about going with the regular text messages or you prefer to have a conversation, these tips would help you manage your fears and then expert navigate your sex conversations.

1. Breathe in and relax

It is understandable that you would immediately tense up when you are in an unfamiliar situation that requires you to be vulnerable. Having a sex talk over the phone whether you are typing or doing the actual calling can put you in a vulnerable place. So, instead of diving in head-first which can cause you to tense up and make the conversation even more awkward than it should be, you should just sit back, take a deep breath and relax. As I always say, you are not being evaluated for your performance or anything. This is an expression of a part of you and it should come just as naturally as you breathing. Of course, we know that nature does not always comply with your demands so you do the next best thing by taking charge of the situation. And as the best psychologists would tell you, you gain control not by holding on but by letting go. Breathe, feel your shoulders relax and then begin.

2. Create an ambiance for the conversation

There is such a thing as setting the mood and it is not just for when you want to have actual physical sex. The idea here is to get you into a comfortable space where you can feel free to lose your inhibitions. With the right lighting and a few upgrades to your decor, your intimate space can go from bedroom to boudoir in seconds and with that, a transformation in your attitude towards this very dirty sex talk you are having. As the lights go dimmer, your voice drops an octave lower without any conscious effort on your part, thus making you sound sexier. Turn the heat up a little with touch up to your outfit. Go all out for this if you are at home. This would inject some life into your performance of your character as this sexy orator. If going all out is causing you to stop in your tracks, that is okay. I have been told that a little bit of clothing can make a huge difference in your delivery of the character.

3. Ask questions

You are not a mind reader and so it would be ludicrous to expect you to know exactly what the person at the other end wants without first asking them. Heck, you would have to put yourself through the wringer to get an idea of what you want (as discussed in the previous chapter). Don't put yourself in a situation where you would have to figure out your partner's needs intuitively. The questions that you ask would also help you clarify limits and boundaries so that you know is acceptable and what isn't. Remember, dirty sex talk is meant to be fun and not hurtful or offensive. If you don't ask questions, without meaning to, you might end up doing exactly that or worse, your partner might do it to you.

4. Don't worry about being silly

Silliness comes with the dirty sex terrain and if you are expecting it to be this serious adult fun type of thing, you may be towing the wrong line. Dirty sex talk would require you to go out of character and do a little acting. Some of it can be...well, silly. And this is okay. The silliness is what makes it fun. Nobody cares about your high-end job as an attorney or sales rep for one of those big brands. Right now, you are naughty Silvia or sexy Steve from the bar or whoever you and your partner have made you become. Commit to the character and play it out even though you may feel a little silly.

5. Have a sense of humor

Laughter can get you out of the tightest spots in life. Viewing your next sexual adventure through your humor lenses can help you get over any awkward silences or challenges that may come up. With a good sense of humor, you can tolerate the silliness and overcome any shyness you might have. Humor may not immediately fix the problem (like your struggle to string sentences together) but it is going to take the edge off you and make you feel less pressured.

Your smartphone can be very instrumental in spicing up your sex life and helping you become better at this whole dirty sex talk thing. You just have to understand the basic rules of engagement. But more than that, you have to understand that this is a fun experience and if all of this is stressing you out, then you are taking things way too seriously. Sure you want to impress your significant other with your witty comebacks, double entendres, and general cleverness, but if you ask most people, they would tell you that the biggest turn on is seeing their partners have fun. So, unplug yourself from all the stress and commit to having fun. You can't go wrong with that.

Chapter Five - Deep in the Dirty Talk

This chapter is all about examples. You have laid the foundation, given yourself the confidence boost that you need and gone over the rules of keeping your relationship healthy and the communication lines clean while you take your sex talk conversation to the filthiest heights. By now, you should know what dirty sex talk isn't. And to honor this amazing progress you have made, we are going to look at what dirty sex talk is. Go over these examples when you are ready to start texting. You can use them as they are or you can modify them to match the mood and your situation. At the end of this chapter, you are going to find out that you have got things under control all along and that there really wasn't any reason to panic. A word of caution though; these messages are going to change your sex life forever. Make sure that this is what you want before you proceed.

30 Dirty Phrases to Instantly Turn Someone On

In this segment, I am going to break this messages into 3 different groups; Level one for the beginner, level two for the sex talker who has gotten over the initial issues but still trying to get comfortable with the sexiness of it all and then you have level three which is where the filthiest conversations happen. Enjoy!

10 level one phrases to turn on the heat

- I cannot wait to see you later tonight. I think we should try something fun. Wink wink

- Baby, I have a very sexy surprise waiting for you when you come over tonight

- I am having trouble concentrating on work today. All I can think about is what we did last night

- I can't stop thinking about you. I still have your scent on me from what we did this morning

- I am lying in bed right now. I am very naked and very horny. Got any ideas?

- I am still sore from everything you did to me last night. I can't wait for a repeat performance

- You were so wet/hard last night. I have never seen you so turned on

- I just got out of the shower. (this should be accompanied by a sultry picture)

- Hey babe, are you going to be home this evening? I am thinking of stopping by and going down on you

- I just found our next assignment. (include a photo of a Kamasutra sex position)

10 level two phrases to stir up the conversation

- I am craving your dick/pussy in my mouth right now. I need to be stuffed

- I am going to be very busy tonight. I plan to spend most of it between your legs

- You taste so good that it is hard to choose between sucking you and fucking you

- When you come over later tonight, I am going to make sure you cum

- I have got everything we need for a night of pleasure. Just bring your dick/pussy and we're good

- When you are dressing up for our date tonight, leave out the underwear. You wouldn't need that for I have planned

- Eat a lot of pineapples and bananas. I am going to be sucking them out of you later

- I love it when you rub my clit as you tuck me from behind

- I want you to dominate me later tonight. Grab my boobs, pinch my nipples, pull my hair and then make me go down on my knees so that you can cum on my face

- I love it when you squeeze your pussy around my dick

10 level three phrases no one can resist

- I am going to put my pussy on your lips and squirt my juices all over your face

- Grind that pussy hard on this cock.

- Open that pretty little mouth and stick that tongue out so that I can spill my cum on it

- Bend over baby. I have a hard dick ready to fuck that wet pussy

- I can't get enough of you sucking my nipples baby

- Your pussy is not the only hole I am going to play with

- Every time I wake up in the morning, the first thing I think about is how hard I want to fuck you

- I want to be your dirty sex whore. Make me you fuck slave

- I want to bury my tongue in your pussy and suck all the juices out of you

- I am not wearing anything under this dress. I can't wait for you to bring out your dick and fuck me

30 Hot and Dirty Questions to Ask Your Partner

One way to get into your partner's mind during sex is by asking questions. However, there are no rules that say you have to be clinical and unfun when you are asking those questions. With the right phrases and a few choice words in your vocabulary, you can stir up the conversation so sweetly that it sets the stage for an epic lovemaking session. In this case, we are not going to look at what level you are on in the dirty sex talk game. These questions cut across the board and can be used for sexting, voice and video calls or even during those private moments you have with each other under the sheets. You can use the questions as they to test your partner's reception to the questions or you can modify them as you see fit.

1. Do you like it when I…(insert the sex act here) like this?
2. What naughty thing would you like me to do to you?
3. How do you want me to fuck you? Fast or slow?
4. Why does your dick/pussy drive me so crazy like this?
5. I am super horny right now, what are you going to do about it?
6. Do you want to watch me get on my knees and suck you?
7. I am missing your delicious cock/pussy. When are you coming home?
8. I want to … (insert a description of the sexual act), are you up for it?
9. How did you know how to do the things that you do to me?

10. When was the last time we did the (insert sexual position)? Care to try?

11. It has been a while since I had an orgasm. When next are you coming?

12. Do you want me to suck your nipples while I play with your pussy?

13. Can I come over to your place right now and fuck you really hard?

14. Last time, we had all kinds of fun toys in our bed with us. I had four orgasms. What are we going to do next?

15. I am fantasizing about your dick inside me, can you make it a reality?

16. Remember that time you sucked my hard dick in a cab?

17. What sex scene from (insert the name of the movie) should we act out tonight?

18. What outfit would you like to see me in when you get home later today?

19. How do you feel when I suck your clit like this?

20. I am fondling your nipples now, would you like me to keep playing with them or should I move on to your pussy?

21. what is your craziest and nastiest sexual fantasy?

22. I am fantasizing about putting my dick in your pussy right now. Can we make that a reality?

23. If you had to choose between oral sex, anal sex, and vaginal sex for the next six months, which one would you go for?

24. Do you like it when I talk dirty in bed?

25. What is the highest number of times you have orgasmed at a go?

26. Would you watch porn with me or would you rather watch me masturbate to porn?

27. Do you have any kinks that involve me being your slave or would you prefer that vice versa?

28. Does anyone around us really know how good you fuck me?

29. What are you doing later tonight? I am thinking we can have a quickie before dinner

30. I have a nice wet pussy for you. Do you want to drive your dick in and fuck me?

Nine Essential Tips for Dirty Talking the Right Way

In the previous chapter, we have looked at how to get started for beginners. We have also gotten into the basic things that you need to know before you unleash your inner freak. Now, we want to look at things you can do to make you sound sexier and in so doing, making your little sex talk so hot that your sheets might as well be on fire. You know that we have already said that dirty sex talk is more than using words that most people do not use in everyday sentences. It is more about how you say it. These tips that I am about to share with you will help you hone your dirty mind for better sex talk.

1. Be sure to turn yourself on

A lot of times, we enter into these conversations because we are hoping to please our sexual partners and not necessarily because we are adventurous. Your partner suggested this new thing for both of you to try and even though it sounds fun, you are not really into it but you do it anyway because you want to make your partner happy. With this kind of attitude, the dirty sex talk thing becomes a chore that you are doing for your partner. If this sounds like you, stop that attitude. To do sex talk right, you need to be turned on and this next tip could help you with that.

2. Customize your erotic adventure

The stuff that we fantasize about may not be mainstream and fearing judgment for our preferences, many of us choose to join the crowd. This decision means you are not really feeding your mind with the kind of things that you genuinely know to make you happy. Sacrificing your pleasure on the altar of conformity might cost you the opportunity to really get down and dirty. You may be straight as an arrow but find that same-sex porn is what turns you on. That doesn't mean that you want to convert. You simply find certain activities very appealing. Own it and if you are going to stream porn, let that be your thing.

3. Let the tenses inspire you

At some point during the conversation, you will get stumped for ideas. While that is perfectly normal, it doesn't have to signal the natural death of that conversation. You can always focus on past tense, present tense or future tense to drive the conversation. Here are a few examples of what I mean:

- **Past tense:** I loved the way sucked my dick the other night.
- **Present tense:** I have a deposition to make but all I am thinking about right now is rubbing my pussy against your tongue
- **Future tense:** The next time I see you, I am going to bend you over and fuck you from behind

4. Be flirty as you get dirty

Dirty sex does not have to mean that flirting goes outside the window. Sometimes, you can get raunchy without having to commit yourself to the process. Allow yourself to enjoy the act of intellectually stimulating your sex life without feeling the obligation to make everything turn into a sexual fantasy every single time. Flirting is good and if that is what you are in the mood for, I say go for it.

5. Have an erotic negotiation

This is particularly important for couples who are just starting out their relationship. Those sultry messages should not have to mean that you compromise in matters that are important to you. For instance, you can express your concerns about your sexual health without having to get all clinical about it. For example, you could say something in the lines of, I want to fuck you so bad right now. Should we grab condoms or would you rather we use pills? In this sentence, you have been able to discuss birth control without having to create a lecture around the subject. Erotic negotiations help you to get what you want and it doesn't always have to be about the sex itself.

6. Stay away from acronyms

This is for when you get to sexting. Using short abbreviations to compose sexts is such a preadolescent thing to do in what is meant to be an adult conversation. You might get away with one or two abbreviations in a text but even at that, the frequency of those texts would affect the flow of the conversation. Besides, nobody wants to spend valuable time decoding your texts. There are acceptable acronyms like LOL, XOXO and OMFG. Limit their use in a sext and you should be fine. But things like l8tr, k and u (instead of you) just don't work.

7. Pay attention to your grammar and punctuation

You are writing an essay so you can heave a sigh of relief right now. However, you have to keep in mind the fact that poor grammar can be a major turn off when you are having a dirty sex talk. Whether you are having phone sex or doing your dirty sex talk, keep the dialogue in acceptable English. Unless of course, you are conversing in your own language. Even then, keep the grammar clean. For texts, use punctuation where it is necessary. Exclamation points have a way of injecting excitement into any conversation. Feel free to use it frequently.

As you keep practicing and putting your dirty mind to work, you would always find ways to tweak the conversation in your favor. Along the way, you would pick up some tips and some tricks of the trade. This would help you be better. Embrace the journey. In the next chapter, we would discuss another exciting aspect of dirty sex talk.

Chapter Six - Roleplay

If you had the chance to someone else other than who you are right now, would you take it? Roleplay gives you the chance to explore your sexual personalities and bring some of your sexual fantasies to life. You assume a character, work out the logistics for getting into that role and then you bring it to life. For a novice, it might seem odd or bizarre even to be anything but ourselves. But without realizing it, a lot of us get into character every day in different situations. This involuntary act is considered an act of self-preservation. There might be several reasons why you choose to get into character. One of them is a fear of criticism. As humans, we are biologically programmed to connect with other people and one way to connect is to act as a group of people. Failure to do so could lead to rejection.

We all remember what high school was like, but that kind of change of behavior in order to conform to a group of people does not end at a certain age or educational stage in class. Even in our very adult lives, we find ourselves switching between characters to suit our "tribe". For example, if you are hanging out with your friends who come from a certain type of background, you would find out you have blended in and you are one of them without question. But the second you come in contact with someone else who may not be in the same group as your friends and comes from a different background, everything changes. When you communicate with this person, you sound different. there would be noticeable differences in your speech, mannerisms, and even facial expressions. Now, it is left to you to decide if you are the real you when you are with the first group of friends or if the one with the second person is your false personality. That is left for you and your shrink to work that out.

This book is not that deep. However, I brought that little nugget of information to help educate you on a natural part of you that you could play up to your advantage especially in the area of sex and that is where role play comes in. With role-play, you can give your sexy dirty talk a lot of variety and dimension. You and your sex partner can become these exciting characters acting out your fantasies and basically being anything but boring. For novices, this is a scary area to get into and not because they are genuinely scared but because of the silliness of it all. Roleplay is like the dress-up thing we used to do as kids. we think of it as talking funny, walking funny and acting funny. But I can tell you (as I am sure anyone who has tried it would tell you), role play is fun but it is sexier than it is funny and this next segment would usher you into this brand new world. You would also be getting pointers on how to make the most of it.

Getting Into Roleplay 101

As with any sexual roleplay, the starting point is your imagination. Set aside any preconceived notions you have about what you think should be considered a normal fantasy and what isn't. Focus on your needs and sexual desires. The ideal sexual role play is born from the parties involved tapping into their inner desires. So, just as you need a little bit of sexual introspective thinking when you get into dirty sex talk for the first time, you also need to apply that process here. Ask yourself questions about your intimate fantasies. What turns you on the most? When you masturbate without any aid, what are the kinds of visual imagery you use to get you to the promised land? Do you fantasize about being a teacher? Or do you fantasize about being the student in that scenario? Some people get off being complete strangers or even vampires. Whatever your kink is, let it play out fully in your mind. Focus on the elements that turn you on and remember those details.

Next, share your fantasies with your partner. Encourage them to share theirs too. There is nothing like a mutual understanding of each other's sexual desires. Be tactful in sharing your fantasies though. While you may have found some kind of safety in your relationship, you have to understand that some information is better shared gently. Do the sharing by first testing the waters to gauge their receptiveness to your erotic fantasies. Say something like, "lately, I can't stop thinking about…" or you could use a direct question. A question that begins with, "how do you feel about…?" is a great way to get an idea about how your partner might feel about your sexual interests without putting you in the spotlight.

After sharing, the next thing to do is to try and get each other on the same page. And you do this by discussing your plans out loud. Get into the details and specifics of your fantasy. Who plays what in the situation and then you should also decide on the location that you want to use. The performance of your roleplay is not limited to the confines of your bedroom. As a matter of fact, it is not limited in any way at all as long as you engage your imagination. The most important thing is to ensure that all facets of this fantasy bring immense pleasure to both of you. If one party must compromise for the other, there has to be 'the agreement' that the next roleplay would be tailored to suit the desires of the compromising party.

Finally, think of how elaborate you want to be with this and commit to it. You could decide to keep it simple which would still offer you a lot of sexual pleasure if you stick to the basic elements of the fantasy. But if you prefer to go all out, there is also a lot of gratification that comes from planning the whole shindig. Not to mention the ultimate pleasure of seeing that fantasy through. Just go with what works for the moment. Be as resourceful and creative as possible. The end result is totally worth it.

10 Steamy Roleplay Ideas

I like to think that you are completely sold on the idea of taking your dirty sex talk and now that you are getting set to begin, I decided to include a few insanely wicked ideas to try out. Remember, you can either keep things simple by sticking to the basics or going all out with the wigs and the fancy outfits. Just make sure that your pleasure is given priority.

1. Be the porn star

This is a chance for you to reenact your favorite scene from that pron movie that turns you on so much. This could be from a sex position or a technique that was used by the original pornstars. Whatever it is, this is a chance for you to get in on that action and not as a spectator this time around. But as a full-time participant. And guess what? At the end of the day, the pleasure is all yours. The only caveat is this; don't play the porn movie and replicate it at the same time. That is just weird and sort of takes away the fun.

2. Show your love for academics

Remember that crush you had on your teacher back in high school? Well, back then there were all kinds of red tapes but now, with your imagination, those red tapes disappear. You could be the teacher or the student. This depends on what your fantasies are. Since it is all roleplay both of you could take turns playing professor/teacher and the student. It is a fun way to revisit the sexual fantasies of your earlier years.

3. The strangers at the bar

This is a classic roleplay scenario for most couples. Remember when you first met your partner? The butterflies in your stomach that made your heart race, the fact that neither of you could keep your hands off each other...those were the good old days. But as the time passed, the butterfly juices settled and I am guessing you miss that spark. Playing strangers at the bar is a great way to start over. Pick up from where you left off where you met or create a whole new script. It is entirely up to you.

4. The high school power couple

In high school hierarchy, the cheerleader and the ball player ranked at the top. Those giddy days of balancing popularity with responsibility and the raging teenage hormones...no wonder school attendees always acted so sex-crazed. Swing into these characters and perhaps, you just might catch the bug and set your sheets on fire. I am sure that at the end of your session, no one will be complaining.

5. The dominant and the submissive

The power play in a relationship can take on a sexy dynamic if it is exploited. If being dominant turns you on, you can take on the role of the aggressor in this situation while your partner becomes the submissive one. If both of you are turned on by the same thing, you would have to take turns in playing the desired role. Just be sure to discuss the terms of the arrangement like how far you want to go into this. Do you want mild pain or do you want to delve into BDSM fully? Is humiliation a part of the deal? What are your limits and more importantly, what is the safe word to use if you have reached those limits?

6. The master and the maid or the mistress and the plumber

This is a slight deviation from the dom/sub route in that things are not as kinky but you still get a kick out of one of you being in charge and the other being completely helpless. The extreme nature of this relationship when doing a master/mistress and servant roleplay is dependent on the two of you. Just ensure that whatever happens is something that the both of you consented to.

7. The sexy stripper and the paying client

You do not need to go into a strip joint to enjoy the experience of having someone you find appealing move and sway seductively on your laps. It can stand in as exotic foreplay that leads to the main action or it could be part of your sexual routine just to spice it up. If you are playing the role of a paying customer, don't forget to bring good tips.

8. The fireman and the damsel in distress

Firemen are hot and it is not just in the physical sense. The idea of having a strapping young man be so giving of his time and life is so seductive. Ladies want to be rescued and even though they don't, they like the idea of a man being strong for them and we know that men want to play heroes. Just keep it sexy and keep it hot.

9. Doctor/Nurse and Patient

This is one of my personal favorites. Mostly because of the exaggerated costumes. The nurse is usually overtly sexy and she has a right to touch you even if you do not want to be touched. And this is part of this roleplaying game that is the most appealing. The doctor, on the other hand, is that sleazy pervert that we want in our beds. The perfect way to explore all your Grey's anatomy fantasies.

10. Your favorite movie duo

Some movies have characters that leave an indelible mark on us and sometimes, those marks are very sexual. Well, here is your chance to rekindle those sexy TV moments on your own terms. You can follow the script to the letter or you can add your own twist to your story. Make things even more interesting.

How to Start Roleplaying Via Text

If you are in a long-distance relationship and you would like to do roleplay with your partner, thankfully, you can still get in on the fun through text messaging. This is a little different from your regular sexts and witty chats over the phone. There is a precision to this kind of text message to enable both of you get into character and bring your fantasies to life. In the next few steps, you will learn exactly how to do it. But before we do that, let us explore the concept a little bit more. As any of us would know, texting is an essential part of a relationship in today's world. It keeps the communication going even when the two of you are far apart and by including roleplay in your communication, you are able to spice up your conversations and give your sex lives a good boost. For couples who are yet to have sex, roleplaying through text messages gives you the opportunity to engage in your sexual fantasies without ever really committing to it. These benefits are just the tip of the iceberg when it comes to sexual roleplay texting. That said, I think the next question would be, how do you bring the magic of sexual roleplay to life when all you have are your phone and your fingers? Well, let us get into that, shall we?

Step one: Talk about it first

You have to come to a mutual understanding about these things before you swing into action. This is not the kind of thing you just throw at your partner and expect them to comply and get into the game without first having an extensive discussion about it. Even if your partner is the happy go lucky type, they still need to understand the script you are presenting to them before they immerse themselves in character. That way, both of you would get a satisfying outcome that would lead to sexual gratification or at the very least, genuine enjoyment of the roleplaying game as it unfolds. Having a conversation about this goes beyond telling your partner what you want. It also means listening to their own needs and working out how to incorporate both of your desires and fantasies into the theme of the game. When both of you are on the same page, the texts become twice as fun.

Step two: Explore all fantasies to find the right one

If that phrase made you feel as though you have fallen into the matrix and you are wondering if you are now talking to the great Morpheus, I can relate. But seriously, this makes a lot of sense. If you have never done roleplay in a sexual capacity before, you may feel unsure as to playing out the right script for the ultimate sexual stimulation. All you have right now are a list of things that turn you on but you have no idea if they would bring about your eventual sexual gratification. I have been on that ledge and I have to say that the only way to know for sure is to take a leap and try them all. Just keep an open mind as you explore. Some of the kinky stuff that you find so appealing might turn out to be a bore when you actually follow through on playing out your fantasy. That should not spell doom for your roleplaying expedition. Simply cross it off your list and move on to the next thing.

Also, remember to pay attention to the elements that did turn you on. There could be some potential there if you follow through on it.

Step three: Create a safe space to explore

None of you should be made to feel like an unwilling participant in this roleplay sexting game… not unless that is your actual thing and if it all, by all means, have fun. That aside, your explorations should be limited to what both of you feel comfortable doing. The second either of you starts feeling out of their depth or way off to the left, there should be a safe-word you can use to alert the other person and put a halt to the fantasy roleplay. This is not about you being a stick in the mud. It is about protecting the integrity of your emotions. Roleplay through texts or any other means does not mean that you are automatically signing away your right to enjoy the game and subject your feelings to the whims of the other person's desires. Again, unless this is something that turns you on (being the sub to a very dominant partner), you don't need to engage in anything that makes you uncomfortable. After tapping out of the game with the safe word that both of you have created, find out what exactly made you feel uncomfortable and then take the time to explain that to your partner. If your partner is the one who initiated the safe word, be understanding and cut things off right away. Do not pressure them to explain their discomfort if they are not ready to. Just be supportive and respect their boundaries.

These are the basic steps to get you started in this direction but you have to understand that you can only really take things to the next level with practice. The communication style that both you and your partner have will go a long way in dictating the direction of these things. So, keep that in mind. And most importantly, if at first, you don't succeed, remember the golden rule of life. dust yourself up and try again. As long as both of you are open to this, you should be able to find what works for you eventually. Regardless of how it plays out, try to ensure that both of you are having fun. That is what we are here about anyway.

Chapter Seven - Other Erotic Exercises

Beyond dirty sex talk and roleplaying, there are tons of other fun activities we can introduce into our sexual relationships to keep the flames burning. But before we get into those (I found some really fun activities), I want to say something that I think may have an impact on the state of things in your sex life. If you find yourself in a place where you are constantly needing to try new things in order to keep the relationship going, there might be foundational elements of a strong relationship missing in yours and this is what is prompting your need to go on the next adventure. If that is the case, I would recommend looking into those missing elements because, while sex is a bonding activity for couples, it does not necessarily become the glue that keeps the two of you together. The sexual activities listed in this book are meant to be that extra sauce that fires up your sex lives and not the bandaid that holds it together.

Now that we have cleared that up, let us look into these cool activities that promise to keep things steamy between you and your sexual partner.

10 Sexy Games to Get in the Mood

If you find your zeal for sex taking a dive, these fun games would awaken you sexually and get things going. Just be warned though, there is a very strong possibility that playing any of these games would have you screaming passionately for more by the end of the night...which is great for every person involved. The best part of these games is the fact that there are no losers here. It is a classic win-win situation for all.

1. Become the card magician

Do you know those magic tricks where the magician asks a member of the audience to pick a card and then does some disappearing and reappearing act that makes the crowd drop their jaws? Well, this is not that game. You and your partner are to take turns picking any card and whatever is on the card would require the other party to perform sexual acts. The acts to be performed would be determined by your interpretation of the symbols on the card. Diamonds could mean oral sex for example and if your partner draws ten of diamonds, you can interpret that to mean, you get 10 minutes of quality oral sex.

2. The orgasm race

This is a contest for who gets to the finish line first without any help from the other person. In other words, both of you would masturbate in front of each other. The winner assists the other person in attaining their orgasm and then proceeding to the next level of the game. Before you get into it, decide on what the rewards would be.

3. Treasure hunt

This is a mental and physical game of X marks the spot. You would ask your partner to guess what part of your body you are thinking about and they are not to say those words verbally. Instead, they are to kiss the spot they think you are thinking about and the only clue that they would get from you are the words, hot or cold. This would continue until they hit the spot and then you swap.

4. The learning game

Put your partner's knowledge of you to the test with this game. Lie in bed wearing the most sultry outfit. Have your partner stand by the door and then ask him or her sexual questions about you. For every answer they get right, they take a step closer to you and you lose and item of clothing. Keep at it until you are completely naked or neither of you can bear the torture.

5. The game of mirrors

Sit down facing each other and then perform sexual activities on your partner and have them perform the exact same move on you. You guys should take turns showing each other these moves and letting the other person replicate them.

6. The no penetration game

Get a timer, set it on for a specific amount of time. At that time, both of you can do all kinds of sexual things to each other. Everything and anything except for penetration. Keep at this until the timer that you have set elapses. Also, you are not allowed to have an orgasm in that time frame either.

7. Get a sex board game

I love monogamy which is the sexy version of monopoly. There are tons of really good sex board games out there. Explore as many as you can and if you can't find one right away, take the regular game that you already have and give it a sexual element just like the card game we just talked about.

8. Good old truth or dare

This is a classic except in this version, the focus is more on the dare than the truth. Dare each other to perform sexual activities in specific ways. Be as creative as possible and don't miss out on the opportunity to indulge in each other's fantasies.

9. The goody bag game

Both of you should look around the house for random objects. Sanitize those objects and then present them to each other in the bedroom. Now the challenge here is really simple, the other party should come up with a way to use the objects presented to bring sexual pleasure to the other person. Let your imagination run wild here. The goal is pure sexual pleasure

10. Naked warfare

I am a big fan of sex and the city and one of my favorite scenes was from when Samantha was having a mock wrestling match with this wrestling trainer. They would tackle each other into a position and just go at it. The adrenaline from the physical contest drives your sexual anticipation off the roof. You can create your own variant of this game by making it a contest for taking off each other's clothes. Do your best to make it difficult for your partner and vice versa.

Less Known but Highly Effective Strategies for Dirty Talk

So far, you have discovered and hopefully learned a lot of things that can improve your sexual relationship. I am also hopeful that there is still enough room in you for you to learn more. We have already discussed extensively on things that you can do to introduce dirty sex talk to both you and your partner. We walked through the baby steps and also got some incredible pointers (if I do say so myself) on how to navigate those unfamiliar terrains and conquering your fears. This segment is very handy for the moment that comes after you have taken those first steps. This segment is no longer about taking the first step but it is about better even better at it. These tips would make you more eloquent in your dirty conversations. Remember, this is not about being perfect. The goal here is to help you maintain an interesting conversation long enough to sexually stimulate both you and your partner. Whether you would be doing the talking via texts or whispering those naughty words in your partner's ears directly, these tips work well.

1. Let the pros inspire you

As I mentioned earlier in the book, porn is not just for sexual gratification. With the right mindset, it could be an educational tool. I used the phrase, "right mindset" because you have to understand what it is you are going to learn from them. In this situation, I would focus on what they say more than how they say it. Those dirty phrases can inspire your lingo when it comes to dirty talk. Not all porn movies feature the heavy use of dirty talk so go for videos where the actors like to verbally engage. When you hear new phrases that pique your interest, quickly write it down and file it away for future use. And before you get you use it, practice with it first. Without practice, when you use those words, they may sound foreign to you and may not pack the sexual punch just yet. Let the words roll of your tongue until it feels natural to you and then give it your twist by using it in your own way. By the time you get to this point, you would have gotten rid of any complexes or awkwardness you may have associated with the phrase and made it your own.

2. Build your vocabulary through body part poetry

Yep. This is actually a thing. You don't just go from point A to point K without going through a process and this is one of those processes that are critical to helping you become a pro at this. Before you start writing out your own Shakespearean sonnets, hear me out. This exercise basically is about helping you become more descriptive. You start by picking out a body part and describing it in vivid detail. If you want to feel more inspired to follow through on this exercise, think about the favorite part of your partner's anatomy and then describe it in a way that you feel best captures your feelings about their body. It would feel a bit strange at first but with practice, that too will pass. Start off by using one word to describe that body part and then make it two words. Keep at it until you can string together sentences that describe that body part. As you build on this, include those phrases you have been learning from the pros into those descriptions. By weaving those dirty phrases in, you take things from that just descriptive phase into something that is sexually explicit.

3. When in doubt, stick to the sequence

Imagine this. You initiated the dirty sex talk conversation and things are going swimmingly well until somewhere along the way, you draw a blank. For the love of sex, you cannot seem to find the right words to say to keep the momentum going and in panic, you freeze. As humiliating as this might feel, this happens to us all. And for the record, it doesn't mean that you suck at this. You just need to practice some more, that's all. Dirty sex talk has a sequence and I talked about it before. You have the past, the present and the future. And as I mentioned before, the past has to do with sexual experiences that both of you have shared before now. The present is focused on what is happening right now and the future has to do with those things you would like to do to them. When you are feeling like you cannot seem to get a word in, draw inspiration from any of these sexual sequences and then lead with that. Whenever I get in that situation, I always break out of it with something like, "talking to you right now is making me so horny that I can't seem to think straight". This buys me time to get over my awkward brain freeze and helps my partner understand some of my hesitations.

4. Create your own dictionary of adjectives

There are words you hear that instantly turns you on. These could be compliments given to you by your sexual partners or words that make you feel 10 times larger than life. Write those words down. Have a sit-down session with your partner and ask them the same questions too. Let those words become a part of your dirty talk vocabulary in addition to what you have already learned so far. It doesn't matter if these words are just regular words like juicy, hard, slippery, turgid and so on. The fact that they have a sexual connotation known to just the two of you should be enough to heat up your conversations.

On a final note, practice is everything. As you build your personal dirty talk dictionary, be sure to put them to use in your sex conversations. The more familiar you become with theses words in sexual contexts, the better you would become at this.

How to Maintain the Spark with Your Partner

At some point in your relationship, the sexual spark is not going to be as hot or as intense as it used to be in its infant days. This could be because one or both parties have allowed other things to take priority over your sexual life. Or perhaps you never had the spark in the first place because you feel that sex is for procreation purposes only. Whatever the reason for the diminishing of the sexual flames, with a little effort from both sides, you can get over this hump and renew your passion for each other. It may not happen overnight but if you are consistent and committed to the process, you will reach your goals eventually.

1. Be on the same page

One person is not always enough to bring back the heat into your sexual relationship. Both of you have to want this and you have to be on the same page on how you go about it. Have a talk with your partner to find out if there are any other emotional or mental roadblocks that might be interfering with your sexual life. This is particularly important for people with a sexual personality that hinges their sexual attraction to their emotional connection to a person. There are so many instances where we suffer sexually because we can't connect emotionally. Figure this out and set things right.

2. Take a class

In this book, you are taking a class on dirty sex talk and you are learning all the amazing ways you can give your sex life a boost with words. There are so many other things you could try out and this time, do it together. Take things to the next level by signing up for physical classes that offer you knew sexual experiences to try out. The bonus is that at the end of the class, you can spend a while practicing all those things that you have learned. So whether it is pole dancing, tantric sex or even bondage for couples, the novelty of learning and trying something new together as a couple can improve the state of things in the bedroom.

3. Go on a short trip together

The introduction to a new environment, as well as the change of pace, has a way of driving two people together. You don't have to go far away at all if you cannot afford it. As a matter of fact, you can have a mini-vacation right in the comfort of your home. Rather than go about your weekend routine, as usual, you can plan on keeping those activities to the bare minimum. Order in to avoid spending time cooking and doing dishes and then invest in a nice erotic book. Take turns reading it out loud to each other and then, act out the scenes that most appeal to you and your partner.

4. Set aside a "sex night"

You schedule date night to spend some time together and while this may sound clinical, you could do yourselves some good if you schedule sex night too. As you probably guessed, sex night is a night dedicated to having sex. Before you protest, let me clear up a few things. Sex night does not mean that you are not permitted to have sex any other night. I know that sex is meant to be a spontaneous thing that happens spur of the moment but here are the things about sex night. This is about the two of you taking the time to explore each other sexually. Sex night is not about the regular routine sex that both of you have. It is more or less a fact-finding mission where both of you make discoveries by trying out new things. Sex night is for creating new sexual experiences.

5. Do something new together

For this exercise, the objective is to carry out activities together that are in no way related to what goes on in the bedroom. This is a non-sexual way to bond with your partner and create new memories. These new memories have a way of bringing the two of you closer. Now, you may not find yourselves ripping each other's clothes off at the end of the day. However, it creates a level of intimacy that will stir things up between the sheets. You can stick to the regular routine activities that you carry out together like cooking, doing the dishes and so on. That is fine but having new activities like tackling a DIY project together is what you need to ignite that spark.

6. Talk to each other

Communication is the bedrock for any relationship. But when a relationship has a sexual element to it, communication is the engine that drives that ship. More often than not, when a relationship tanks sexually, the root cause is usually a breakdown in communication. When the walls come up and no one is willing to talk to each other, you have a problem. Another issue is when both of you are talking but no one is listening. That is like attempting to fetch water from the pool using a basket. Everything just drains out. Proper communication involves a lot of talking and listening. Most importantly, both of you have to work hard at creating a healthy environment for communication. A healthy environment is one that is free of judgment, ridicule, and entitlement. It should be nurturing, respectful and uplifting.

7. Talk to an expert

When you find that both of you are unable to have a conversation with each other, the next best thing is to talk to someone else. A mediator of some sorts who would help the two of you bridge the gaps emotionally, mentally and sexually. A trained relationship counselor can help you get over any hurdles in your relationship by highlighting the problematic areas and proffering practical solutions that would bring the two of you together to the same page. They are all about building the intimacy between couples which in turn, enhances their sex lives.

Conclusion

I think I started writing this book years before the thought of putting it down for print even occurred to me. I was years into my relationship at the time and we had hit a rut in our sex lives. I was desperately looking for ways to bring back some of the old flames into our sex routines which were practically non-existent at the time. Sadly, I was unable to save that relationship but I did learn something valuable that changed my life. Dirty talk is amazing and I loved it. And I am hoping that you would love it and make it a part of you too.

I am truly honored to have been a part of your journey to understanding the concept of dirty talk. We may call it dirty talk but by now I am hoping that you are aware that there is nothing dirty about enhancing your sexual experiences by being a little more verbally invested. Beyond that, this book also guides you towards your deepest sexual desires. Rather than hide behind a facade to mask your true emotions, this book is about exploring them but not just on your own. You have to do it with your partner as well. I think one of my biggest lessons on the subject learning to take charge of one's own orgasm. You cannot keep waiting for other people to please you if you will not first, find a way to please yourself.

There may be a lot of things you don't have control over and your sex life is not one of them. In this book, you are urged to take the time to explore your body and your sexual needs. This is based on the understanding that sex is a beautiful and very important part of our biological makeup. Sex brings about procreation but it also serves to bring you pleasure. On this journey that you have taken, strive to have an intimate relationship with yourself before you start looking out for anybody. This is not because you are trying to be selfish. As a matter of fact, the more knowledgeable you are about your sexual needs, the more capable you become of bringing pleasure to other people.

Free yourself of the burdens of any preconceived notions you have about sex. focus on what is happening right now. Understand your sexual personality so that you can understand your reaction to certain things. While the expected outcome of your foray into is an amazing sex life afterward, you have to remind yourself that there are certain holes in a relationship that sex cannot fill. So, while you are doing this, don't neglect those other aspects of your relationship in the hopes that this will be a quick fix. That said, the things that you learn in this book is going to make a lot of difference. Thankfully, I have walked in your shoes before as a novice and I perfectly understand the challenges associated with this.

And it is for this reason that I included over 100 examples to help you get started on your journey to becoming a seasoned professional on the subject while sparing you from having to go through those terrible experiences first hand. I even got a few tips from people who do the dirty talk for a living. and to wrap things up, we also explored some other ways to spice up your sex life and now, we have come to the end of this book. But before I run off into the sunset, I wanted to leave you with these words of wisdom. The end of the book does not have to mean the end even though it has that ring of finality to it. This is the commencement of a new chapter in your life. One where there are a lot of possibilities and potentials. Explore the knowledge that you have gained here to the fullest. As you grow, do some of your own research and then take pointers from the lessons you have learned on this journey to self-discovery. Continue building your confidence as you overcome your fears.

Every time you feel lost along the way, go back to the previous chapters you have read. Let the words inspire you to be a better and more exciting lover. Also, remind yourself that failure does not really mean the end of the road either. I know that I have talked about this more than once in the book but I am bringing it here again because this is a very important truth. There is no such thing as perfection. This is about having fun and enjoying the process. Just know that as long as you keep practicing, you will become a pro in no time. The second thing that I hope stays with you as you move forward with the knowledge that you have gained is the fact that communication is the key. You don't just spring these details on your partner. You don't just wake up and decide that roleplay and dirty talk are what you want to do and for that reason, they have to get on board.

Share your thoughts, share your desires and better still, share your need to bring more passion and excitement into your relationship. Sharing is an important element to this whole process and you do it by communicating. And finally, I want to celebrate your courage for taking on this challenge and to say congratulations on making it this far. I am even more excited about where this is going to take you.

I wish you nothing but the best dear reader!

www.ingramcontent.com/pod-product-compliance
Lightning Source LLC
Chambersburg PA
CBHW030347100526
44592CB00010B/857